J. D. (Josiah Dwight) Whitney

The Yosemite Guidebook

A Description of the Yosemite Valley and the Adjacent Region of the Sierra Nevada,

and of the Big Trees of California

J. D. (Josiah Dwight) Whitney

The Yosemite Guidebook
A Description of the Yosemite Valley and the Adjacent Region of the Sierra Nevada, and of the Big Trees of California

ISBN/EAN: 9783744662833

Printed in Europe, USA, Canada, Australia, Japan

Cover: Foto ©Andreas Hilbeck / pixelio.de

More available books at **www.hansebooks.com**

GEOLOGICAL SURVEY OF CALIFORNIA.

J. D. WHITNEY, State Geologist.

THE

YOSEMITE GUIDE-BOOK:

A DESCRIPTION OF THE YOSEMITE VALLEY AND THE
ADJACENT REGION OF THE SIERRA NEVADA,
AND OF THE BIG TREES OF CALIFORNIA,

ILLUSTRATED BY MAPS AND WOODCUTS.

PUBLISHED BY AUTHORITY OF THE LEGISLATURE.

1869.

UNIVERSITY PRESS: WELCH, BIGELOW, & CO.,
CAMBRIDGE.

TABLE OF CONTENTS.

CHAPTER I.

INTRODUCTORY.

Object of the present volume, — its origin, — the Congressional grant of the Yosemite Valley and the Big Trees to the State of California, 9 ; action of the Governor, — appointment and names of Commissioners, — surveys to establish the boundaries of the grants, — acceptance of the grants by the State, 10 ; action of the Legislature, — authority given the State Geologist to prepare a guide-book of the Valley and Grove, — action of the Commissioners and the State Geologist in carrying out the directions of the Legislature, 11 ; Surveys made for the Commissioners, — report of the Commissioners, 13 ; their plans and wishes, — history of the settlement of the Yosemite Valley, — Indian war, 14 ; aboriginal names of the prominent points in and around the Yosemite, 16, 17 ; these names not current at present, — system adopted by the Geological Survey in giving names, 18 ; history of the discovery and settlement of the Yosemite, — first visits by tourists, — public houses built there, 19 ; settlers in the Valley, — their attempt to get possession of it, — action of the Legislature and Congress, 20 ; reason for not yielding to their demands, 21 ; the promises and the duties of the State of California, 22.

CHAPTER II.

GENERAL.

Sketch of the topographical features of the United States, 24, 25 ; the mountain system west of the 105th meridian, 25 ; the name suggested for it as a whole, 26 ; history of its exploration, 26, 27 ; need of good maps, — sanitary value of mountain travel, 27 ; mountains of California, 28 ; the Coast Ranges and the Sierra Nevada, 29 ; topography and botany of the Coast Ranges, 31, 33 ; interesting points to be visited, 34, 35 ; ascent of Monte Diablo, 34 ; character of Coast Range scenery, 35 ; views from points about San Francisco, 35, 36 ; the Sierra Nevada, 37–46 ; its extent, 37 ; elevation, 38 ; heights of passes and dominating peaks, 38, 39 ; its geology, 39 ; forest vegetation, 40, 41 ; climate, 42 ; rain and snow on the Sierra, 43, 44 ; former existence of glaciers, 45 ; former greater precipitation, 46.

CHAPTER III.

THE YOSEMITE VALLEY.

The Yosemite Valley, its position, 47; routes to, 48; advantages of each, 49; advice in regard to getting to and from the Valley, 50; the route by Coulterville, 51; the Bower Cave, 52; Pilot Peak, 53; route by Bear Valley and Mariposa, 54; White and Hatch's, — Clark's ranch, 55; Westfall's, — position of the Yosemite, — maps referred to, 56, 57: principal features of the Valley, 57; El Capitan, 58; Bridal Veil Fall, 59; Virgin's Tears Fall, — Cathedral Rock, 60; the Three Brothers, 62; Sentinel Rock, 62; the Yosemite Fall, 62 – 65; Royal Arches, — North Dome, 66; Half Dome, 67, 68; Mirror Lake, — Cloud's Rest, 69; the Vernal Fall, 70; Nevada Fall, 71; the Illilouette cañon, 72; botany, topography, and geology of the Yosemite, 72 – 87; its shape and elevation, 73; vegetation, 73 – 76; the walls, — exit from, 77; its waterfalls, 77; changes in the waterfalls at different seasons, 78; comparison of celebrated falls with those of the Yosemite, 79; appearance of the Valley in the winter, — peculiar type of scenery in the Yosemite, 80; how originated, — not by aqueous erosion, 81, 82; nor by glaciers, 83; general remarks on the formation of Valleys, 84; theory suggested for the origin of the Yosemite, 85; reasons for adopting this theory, 86, 87.

CHAPTER IV.

THE HIGH SIERRA.

Visitors to the Yosemite advised to extend their journey to the higher regions of the Sierra Nevada, — advantages of the climate for such excursions, 88; comparison of Swiss and Californian scenery, 89; tour around the Yosemite, 90; route to be followed, 91; visit to the top of the Three Brothers, 92; to summit of Mount Hoffmann, 93; view of Castle Peak, 93; Lake Tenaya, 94; Cathedral Peak, 95, 96; Tuolumne Valley, and Soda Springs, 97; view from Soda Springs, 98; glaciers once existing here, — description of the scenery, — the Tuolumne cañon probably containing grand waterfalls, — the Hetch-Hetchy Valley, 99; ascent of Mount Dana, 100; topography of the crest of the Sierra, 101; passes near Mount Dana, — view from its summit, 102; geology, — glaciers, — moraine lakes, 103; ascent of Mount Lyell, 104; return route, — the Little Yosemite, 105; Mount Starr King, — Sentinel Dome, 106; views from the Dome and Glacier Point, 107; the Merced Group, — the Obelisk, 108; Mount Ritter, 109; the Hetch-Hetchy Valley, 110, 111; High Sierra at head of King's and Kern Rivers, 112, 138; party for its exploration in 1864, 112; their route, — ascent of Bald Mountain, 113; scenery of the region, — Dyke Ridge, — Big Meadows, 114; Dome Mountains, 115; structure of the granite, 116; the Kettle, 117, 118; the divide beyond the Kettle, 119; Sugar Loaf Rock, — Mount Brewer, 120; view from Mount Brewer, 121, 122; topography of the region, 122; magnificence of the scenery, and character of the country about the head of King's River, 123; Mr. King's ascent of Mount Tyndall, 124, 126; view from its summit, 126; attempt to ascend Mount Whitney, 127, 128; route followed, — topography of the region, — elevation reached, 128 ; cañon of south fork of King's River, 129 ; stupendous scenery, 129, 130; pass out from the cañon, — attempts to reach Mount Goddard, 130; Mount King, 130; the Palisades, 131 ; the party descends into Owen's Valley, 132; return across the Sierra at head of west branch of Owen's River, 133 ; grandeur of the scenery, — Red Slate Peaks, 134 ; depression at forks of King's River, — region loved by the Diggers, 135; ascent of Mount Goddard, — north fork of the San Joaquin, 136 ; dome of granite, — getting out of the cañon, — scenery, — Mount Ritter, 137 ; ascent of Black Mountain, return to Clark's ranch, 138.

CHAPTER V.

THE BIG TREES.

First discovery of the Big Trees, 139 ; history of their scientific nomenclature, 140, 141 ; wide distribution of the cultivated trees, 141 ; name of the genus, whence derived, 141, 142 ; geographical range and habitat of the redwood and Big Tree, 142 ; size of the redwood, 143 ; grandeur of the redwood forests, 144 ; distribution of the Big Trees, 144, 145; the Calaveras Grove, 145 ; measurements of the trees in the grove, 146 ; age of the Big Trees, 147 ; height of, — the Beaver Creek Grove, — the Crane Flat Grove, 148 ; the Mariposa Grove, 149 – 151 ; measurements of trees in this grove, — vegetation of the meadows and grove, 151 ; the Lower Grove, — the Grizzly Giant, — Fresno County Grove, 152 ; the King's River belt of Big Trees, 153 ; the Tule River Groves, 154 ; comparison of the Big Trees with other trees, 154, 155.

PREFATORY NOTE.

A STATEMENT of the way in which the present volume came to be authorized by the Legislature, and of the sources from which the information it contains was drawn, will be found in the introductory chapter. It may be proper to add, that two editions of the work have been published, one in quarto form, with photographic illustrations, the other (the present volume, namely), with woodcuts. These cuts have been selected from among those used in the first volume of our "Geology of California." The maps are the same in both editions, and the text also, except that some verbal changes have been made, and a few pages added, in this edition, relating to that portion of the High Sierra which lies near the head of the Kern, King's, and San Joaquin Rivers.

J. D. W.

CAMBRIDGE, MASS., May 1, 1869.

THE YOSEMITE GUIDE-BOOK.

CHAPTER I.

INTRODUCTORY.

The object of this volume is to call the attention of the public to the scenery of California, and to furnish a reliable guide to some of its most interesting features, namely, the Yosemite Valley, the High Sierra in its immediate vicinity, and the so-called "Big Trees." Much has indeed already been published in regard to these remarkable localities; but in all that has been given to the public, with the exception of the necessarily brief description in the Report of the Geological Survey (Geology, Vol. I.), there has been little of accuracy, and almost nothing of permanent value.

The origin of the present volume is to be found in the action of Congress and the State of California in regard to the Yosemite Valley and the Mariposa Grove of Big Trees. This action dates back to the year 1864. In that year Congress, being moved thereto by certain influential and intelligent citizens of California, passed the following Act:—

"*Be it enacted by the Senate and House of Representatives of the United States of America, in Congress assembled,* That there shall be, and is hereby, granted to the State of California, the 'Cleft' or 'Gorge' in the Granite Peak of the Sierra Nevada Mountain, situated in the county of Mariposa, in the State aforesaid, and the head-waters of the Merced River, and known as the Yosemite Valley, with its branches and spurs, in estimated length fifteen miles, and in average width one mile back from the main edge of the precipice, on each side of the valley, with the stipulation, nevertheless, that the said State shall accept this grant upon the express conditions that the premises shall be held for public use, resort, and recreation; shall be inalienable for all time; but leases not exceeding ten years may be granted for portions of said premises. All incomes derived from leases of privileges to be expended in the preservation and improvement of the property, or the roads leading thereto; the boundaries to be established at the cost of said State by the United States Surveyor-General of California, whose official plat, when affirmed by the Commissioner of the General Land Office, shall constitute the evidence of the locus, extent, and limits of the said Cleft or Gorge; the premises to be managed by the Governor of the State, with eight other Commissioners, to be appointed by the Executive of California, and who shall receive no compensation for their services.

"SECT. 2. *And be it further enacted,* That there shall likewise be, and there is hereby, granted to the said State of California, the tracts embracing what is known as the 'Mariposa Big Tree Grove,' not to exceed the area of four sections, and to be taken in legal subdivisions of one-quarter section each, with the like stipulations as expressed in the first section of this Act as to the State's acceptance, with like conditions as in the first section of this Act as to inalienability, yet with the same lease privileges; the income to be expended in the preservation, improvement, and protection of the property, the premises to be managed by Commissioners, as stipulated in the first section of this Act, and to be taken in legal subdivisions as aforesaid; and the official plat of the United States Surveyor-General, when affirmed by the Commissioner of the General Land Office, to be the evidence of the locus of the said Mariposa Big Tree Grove."

The above-cited Act was approved by the President, June 30, 1864, and shortly after a Proclamation was issued by the then Governor of California, F. F. Low, taking possession of the tracts thus granted, in the name and on behalf of the State, appointing commissioners to manage them, and warning all persons against trespassing or settling there without authority, and especially forbidding the cutting of timber and other injurious acts.

The Commissioners first appointed were F. Law Olmsted, J. D. Whitney, William Ashburner, I. W. Raymond, E. S. Holden, Alexander Deering, George W. Coulter, and Galen Clark, all of whom continue to hold office, with the exception of Mr. Olmsted, who resigned shortly after returning to the East, and whose place has been filled by the appointment of Henry W. Cleaveland.

The surveys necessary to establish the boundaries of the grants in question, as required by the Act of Congress, were made in the autumn of 1864, by Messrs. J. T. Gardner and C. King, and the official plat of their work was forwarded by the Surveyor-General of California to the authorities at Washington, and accepted by the Commissioner of the General Land Office; thus, in the language of the Act, establishing "the locus, extent, and limits" of the grants of the Yosemite Valley and the Mariposa Big Tree Grove.

INTRODUCTORY.

A map of the Yosemite Valley, on a scale of two inches to one mile, was drawn by Mr. Gardner, showing the boundaries of the Yosemite Valley grant, and the topography of its immediate vicinity. This map has been engraved and is appended to the present volume, as will be noticed further on.

Before, however, the Yosemite Valley and the Big Tree Grove could become the property of the State, it was necessary that the grant made by Congress should be accepted by the State Legislature, with all the stipulations and reservations contained therein. The grant had no validity until the State, through its Legislature, had solemnly promised to take the premises for the benefit of the people, for their use, resort, and recreation, and especially "TO HOLD THEM INALIENABLE FOR ALL TIME." This was not an ordinary gift of land, to be sold and the proceeds used as desired; but a trust imposed on the State, of the nature of a solemn compact, forever binding after having been once accepted. Had the State declined to accept the trust, on the conditions expressed in the Act, the whole proceeding would have been null and void, and the premises would have continued, as they originally were, a part of the national domain.

But, at the next session of the Legislature of California after the passage of the Act of Congress cited above, an Act was passed accepting the grant of the Yosemite Valley and the Big Tree Grove, on the stipulated conditions, confirming the appointment of the Commissioners, organizing them into a body for legal purposes, and empowering them to make regulations and by-laws for their own government. The Act of the Legislature also contained provisions making it a penal offence to commit depredations on the premises, and authorizing the appointment of a guardian to take charge of the Grove and Valley.

In this Act there was special authority given to the State Geologist to make further explorations and surveys in and about the premises ceded by the United States, and to prepare and publish such topographical maps and reports on the region as he might deem advisable, for the purpose of furnishing travellers with desirable information. This was a part of the legitimate work of the Geological Survey; and similar explorations, maps, and reports of the whole of the mountain regions of the State, but especially of the Sierra Nevada, should be made, and, indeed, would have been, had the necessary means been furnished by the Legislature; for no more suitable way of employing our time and money could be suggested than this. Thus the first step towards increasing the facilities of travel and fulfilling the stipulations of the grant was taken, to be followed, it was hoped, by opening roads and trails in and about the Valley and Grove, building bridges, and by a variety of similar enterprises calculated to render the region accessible and attractive to travellers.

In obedience to the special request of the Legislature, therefore, our attention was at once turned to the region of the Yosemite Valley; and, as early in 1866 as the season would permit, a party was organized by the State Geologist for the purpose of making a detailed geographical and geological survey of the High Sierra in that vicinity,—a district which had been rapidly reconnoitred and roughly mapped by us during the season of 1863, enough work having been done at that time to satisfy us that its scenery was in the highest degree attractive, and that it possessed many features which should make it particularly desirable as a resort for pleasure travellers, in addition to the Yosemite Valley and the Big Trees themselves. The party of 1866 consisted of Messrs. King, Gardner, Bolander, and Brinley, with two men, and was accompanied during a part of the time by the State Geologist. This party continued in the field from June to October, exploring and mapping the region about the heads of the Merced, Tuolumne, and San Joaquin Rivers, or that portion of the High Sierra which lies between the parallels of 37° 30′ and 38°, and which is most easily and naturally accessible by the same approaches which lead to the Yosemite Valley. An accurate topographical map of the district embraced in these explorations was commenced by Mr. Gardner, in the winter of 1866, on a scale of two miles to one inch. To complete the surveys necessary for this map,—a work requiring more than one season,—another party was organized in 1867, under the direction of Mr. Hoffmann. This party continued in the field during the months of August and September of that year, and the map was finished and placed in the engraver's hands in the spring of 1868, and will be found appended to the present volume. It contains the minute details of the topography of one of the roughest and most elevated portions of the State, and is believed to be the first accurate map of any high mountain region ever prepared in the United States.

Besides the surveys and explorations mentioned above as having been made under the direction of the State Geologist, by authority of the Legislature, for the purpose of preparing a reliable guide-book to the Yosemite Valley, a careful survey of the bottom of the Valley was made for the use of the Commissioners and plotted on a scale of ten chains to one inch, making a map fifty by thirty inches in size. This map has the number of acres of each tract of meadow, timber, and fern land designated on it, and also the boundaries of the claims of the settlers, and a statement of the number of acres enclosed and claimed by them. The principal grove of trees in the Big Tree grant was also surveyed, each tree of over one foot in diameter measured, and the height of a number of them accurately determined. As thus measured, the trees were carefully plotted, so that their exact position, size, and relations to each other can be seen at a glance.

From the very limited appropriation of $2,000 made by the Legislature of 1865–66 for the purposes of the Commissioners, but little remained after paying the salary of the Guardian of the Grove and Valley, Mr. Galen Clark; with what was left some improvements were made on the trails in the Valley, in order to render interesting points more accessible, and two bridges were built across the Merced River; one at the lower end of the Valley, in order to avoid the delay and expense of the ferry; the other above the Vernal Fall, so that the summit of the Nevada Fall might be rendered accessible. Unfortunately, both these bridges were swept away by the unprecedentedly high water of the winter of 1867–68, which destroyed every bridge on the Merced River.

At the session of the Legislature of California which commenced in December, 1867, the first after the taking possession of the Yosemite Valley by the State, the Commissioners presented their report, as required by law, in which they stated what they had been able to accomplish in the way of improvements in and about the Valley, and requested a small additional appropriation for the purpose of making interesting points more accessible, and of removing all charges or tolls on ladders, ferries, bridges, &c. They also asked for a sufficient sum for the salary of the Guardian and his assistant, so that one or the other might be able to be on the spot during all the season for visitors, it having been found that careless or malicious persons would injure or even cut down the trees and shrubs, or set them on fire, unless some person, armed with the authority of the State, was at hand to prevent such mischief.

Besides all this, reference was made to the case of certain settlers in, and claimants to, portions of the Yosemite Valley, to which the attention of the reader will have to be called for a short time. And, in order to understand the condition of things, it will be necessary to go back and give a brief account of the discovery and occupation of the Valley, embodying in this account some particulars with which it will always be interesting for travellers to be acquainted.

The whites living on the streams which head in the vicinity of the Yosemite had, in 1850, found themselves unable to live in peace with the few scattered Indians in that region, and, after some murders and much trouble, a military company was formed to drive them out of the country. In the course of the skirmishing and fighting which took place, it was ascertained that the Indians had a stronghold or retreat far up in the mountains, in which they thought that they could take refuge, and remain without the slightest danger of being found. This place of refuge was the Yosemite Valley, and this was the way in which it first came to be heard of by white people. Of course the curiosity of the settlers was excited in regard to this stronghold, and in the spring of 1851 an expedition was organized, under the command of Captain Boling, to explore the mountains and discover and drive out the Indians from their fastness. This was in March, 1851. Under the guidance of an old chief, named Tenaya, whose name is perpetuated in the beautiful lake which lies between Mt. Hoffmann and Cathedral Peak, and in the branch of the Merced River heading in that lake, the party reached the Valley, drove out the Indians, killed a few, and "made peace" with the rest, who were terribly disheartened at this unceremonious invasion, on the part of the whites, into what they had supposed to be their impregnable retreat. Everything seems to have remained quiet in the region until 1852, when a party of miners was attacked, under what provocation is not stated, by the Indians in the Valley, and two of them killed and buried near the Bridal Veil Meadow. This led to another expedition into the Valley by the Mariposa battalion, who killed some and drove out the rest of the Indians; these took refuge with the Monos, on the eastern side of the Sierra, but got into difficulty there, and, escaping with a lot of stolen horses, were followed back to the Yosemite by the Monos, where a battle was fought resulting in the almost entire extermination of the Yosemite tribe. Since that time the Valley has been annually visited by the Monos at the time of the ripening of the acorns, for the purpose of laying in a stock of this staple article of food; but the number of Indians actually and permanently resident in and about the Yosemite or the Mariposa Grove is very small. Like the rest of the so-called "diggers" in California, they are a miserable, degraded, and fast-disappearing set of beings, who must die out before the progress of the white man's civilization, and for whom there is neither hope nor chance.

The Indian residents in and about the Yosemite Valley are said to have been a mixed race, made up of the disaffected of the various tribes from the Tuolumne to King's River.* But little is known of their language; but it is well ascertained that they had a name for every meadow, cliff, and waterfall in and about the Valley. The families of the tribe had each its special "reservation" or tract set apart for its use, each of these, of course, having its distinct appellation. It were much to be desired that these names could be retained and perpetuated, but it is impossible; they have already almost passed into oblivion. They are so long, so uncertain in their spelling and meaning, that they have never been adopted into general use, and never will be. The only one which is current is that of the Valley itself, — "Yosemite," and this, it appears, is not the name given to the Valley by the Indians; the word means "Grizzly Bear," and was probably the name of a chief of the tribe; or, perhaps, this was the name given to the Valley by the band of Indians driven out by the whites in 1851. Such would seem to be the case, from the fact that the name became current at that time. At all events, it is well known that the present Indian name of the Valley is, not Yosemite, but Ahwahnee.

While our party was at the Yosemite, in 1866, the services of a person designated as the most reliable Indian interpreter in the region were secured to accompany us around the Valley and give the Indian names of the different objects and localities and their meaning. This gentleman, Mr. B. B. Travis, furnished the following names, which were taken down by Mr. Bolander as nearly as he could imitate them, the Italian sounds being given to the vowels: —

---

* See Dr. Bunnell's account of the "Indian War" in Hutchings's California Magazine, and in the "Scenes in California," by the same author.

Patéea. The mountain over which the Yosemite trail runs.

Topinémete. The rocks between the foot of the Mariposa trail and the Bridal Veil Fall; said to mean "a succession of rocks."

Póhono. The Bridal Veil Fall; explained to signify a blast of wind, or the night-wind, perhaps from the chilliness of the air occasioned by coming under the high cliff and near the falling water, or possibly with reference to the constant swaying of the sheet of water from one side to the other under the influence of the wind. Mr. Hutchings, more poetically, says that "Pohono" is "an evil spirit, whose breath is a blighting and fatal wind, and consequently to be dreaded and shunned."

Kosúkong. The rocks near Cathedral Rock, sometimes called "The Three Graces."

Pútputon. The meadow and little stream, on the Coulterville trail, first met in coming into the Valley; means the "bubbling of water."

Keialaura. Mountains west of El Capitan.

Lungyotuckoya. The Virgin's Tears Creek, meaning, Pigeon Creek.

Totokónula. Usually spelt Tutocanula, the rock generally called "El Capitan"; the Indians say that this name is an imitation of the cry of the crane, given because, in winter, this bird enters the Valley generally by flying over that rock. How the name El Capitan, the captain, originated it is not easy to say; perhaps it may have been given with the feeling that it was the most striking and impressive mass of rock in the Valley, and the Indians, who often have a smattering of Spanish, may have called attention to it as "el Capitan"; or, as we might say, "the biggest fellow of them all." The west side of El Capitan is called "*Ajema,*" or manzanita, that being a place where they gather the berries of this familiar shrub.

Wawhawke. The Three Brothers; said to mean "falling rocks." The usual name given as that of the Three Brothers is "Pompompasus," equivalent to "Kompopaise" given by our interpreter as the name of the small rock a little to the west of the Three Brothers. It was said to mean "Leaping Frog Rock." The Three Brothers have a vague resemblance to three frogs with their heads turned in one direction, each higher than the one in front. The common idea is, that the Indians imagined the mountains to be playing "Leap Frog." It would remain, in that case, to show that the Indians practise that, to us, familiar game; we have never caught them at it.

Posinaschucka. Cathedral Rock, a large "cache" of acorns; evidently from its shape resembling that of a large stack or cache of acorns, which the Indians are accustomed to build in the trees, in order to secure their stock of food from the depredations of wild animals.

Loya. Sentinel Rock; means an Indian camp, or signal-station, probably.

Ollenya. Small stream between the Three Brothers and the Yosemite Fall; means Frog Brook.

Scholollowi. Indian Cañon; the gulch between the Yosemite Falls and the North Dome.

Ummo. Rocks between the Yosemite Falls and Indian Cañon; means "lost arrow."

Lehamete. Rocks next east of Indian Cañon; meaning, the place where the arrow-wood grows.

Tokoya. The North Dome; meaning, the basket, so named on account of its rounded basket shape.

Schokoni. The Royal Arches; meaning, the shade or cover to an Indian cradle-basket, the shape of these rocks being somewhat like that of this aboriginal and domestic article.

Waiya. Mirror Lake.

Tesaiyak. The Half Dome, generally spelt Tisayac.

Waijau. Mount Watkins; meaning, the Pine Mountain.

Patillima. Glacier Point.

Tululowehäck. The cañon of the South Fork of the Merced, called the Illilouette in the California Geological Report, that being the spelling given by Messrs. King and Gardner,—a good illustration of how difficult it is to catch the exact pronunciation of these names. Mr. Hutchings spells it Tooluluwack.

Peiwayak. The Vernal Fall; meaning, white water; spelt Piwyack by some. Said also to mean sparkling water, or, more poetically, "a shower of crystals"; this is the translation of the word Piwyack given by Mr. Cunningham, from whom the Indian names for objects in and about the Valley have, heretofore, been mostly obtained.

Scholuck. The Nevada Fall, as given by our interpreter. By others this word, or Choolook, as it is often spelt, is used for the Yosemite Fall, while Yowiye is used for the Nevada. Perhaps the word "Scholuck" means simply a waterfall. Yowiye is translated by Mr. Cunningham as meaning "squirming" or "twisted," in reference to the peculiar shape of the Nevada Fall. The discrepancies between the statements of the different interpreters it is beyond our power to reconcile.

A comparison of the above names with those previously published shows how difficult it is to get at the real truth where Indian words and their pronunciation are concerned. As will be noticed, the very name of the Valley itself is uncertain, both as to its origin and orthography. The word "Yosemite" means "a full-grown grizzly bear," and is not that by which the Valley is at present designated by the Indians; and how it is that Ahwahnee, or Auwoni, the real name, failed to be brought into use, it is now impossible to say. Nor is it of much consequence, unless it be to the special student of the aboriginal Indian languages. The names given by the early white visitors to the region have entirely replaced the native ones; and they are, in general, quite sufficiently euphonious and proper. Some of them, perhaps, slightly incline to sentimentality; for if we recognize the appropriateness of the "Bridal Veil" as a designation for the fall called Pohono by the Indians, we fail to perceive why the "Virgin's Tears" should be flowing on the opposite side of the Valley. The Geological Survey has made no changes in the nomenclature either in or about the Valley. We have adopted all the names which were in well-established use, and added nothing. Only in the High Sierra, among the numerous high peaks previously without appellations, we have selected a few, to which we have given the names of some of the most eminent explorers, geographers, and geologists of this and other countries, as will be seen further on in this volume or on reference to the map. This we have done, not so much from any desire to impose designations of our own selection on the public, but because the dominant peaks, such as are necessarily selected for topographical stations, were unnamed, and it would have been excessively inconvenient for us, in plotting our work and describing the country, to be obliged to designate them by numbers. We claim, however, a full and ample right, as the first explorers, describers, and mappers of the High Sierra, to give such names as we please to the previously unnamed peaks which we locate; and the names thus given by us will be adopted by the civilized and scientific world abroad, however much our disinclination to bestow on prominent points the names of great politicians and editors may be criticised in California.*

To return to the subject of the history of the discovery and settlement of the Yosemite Valley. The visit of the soldiers under Captain Boling led to no immediate results in this direction. Some stories told by them on their return found their way into the newspapers; but it was not until four years later that, so far as can be ascertained, any persons visited the Valley for the purpose of examining its wonders, or as regular pleasure travellers. It is, indeed, surprising that so remarkable a locality should not sooner have become known; one would suppose that accounts of its cliffs and waterfalls would have spread at once all over the country. Probably they did circulate about California, and were not believed, but set down as "travellers' stories." Yet these first visitors seem to have been very moderate in their statements, for they spoke of the Yosemite Fall as being "more than a thousand feet high," thus cutting it down to less than one half its real altitude.†

Mr. J. M. Hutchings, having heard of the wonderful Valley, and being, in 1855, engaged in getting together materials to illustrate the scenery of California, for the California Magazine, collected a party and made the first regular tourists' visit to the Yosemite during the summer of that year. This party was followed by another from Mariposa, the same year, consisting of sixteen or eighteen persons. The next year (1856) the regular pleasure travel commenced, and the trail on the Mariposa side of the Valley, from White and Hatch's, was opened by Mann Brothers, at a cost of about $ 700. This trail was afterwards purchased for $ 200 by the citizens of the county, and made free to the public.

---

* The principles we have followed in this Geological Survey, in giving names to prominent natural objects, and especially mountains, which had previously been unnamed, are simple, and such as must commend themselves to all reasonable people. We have selected for this purpose the names of explorers, surveyors, geographers, geologists, and engineers, and especially of such as have worked or lived in the region in which the point to be named was situated. When there was no such name to be found, or when, if found, it was already in use elsewhere, we have, in a few cases, selected, *honoris causa*, the names of very eminent geographers, geologists, or physicists, who have labored successfully in general science, and whose results have thus become the property of the world.

† An article in the Country Gentleman, for October 9, 1856, gives an account of the Yosemite Valley, in which the heights of several points are given with an approach to accuracy; this article, which professes to be based on one in the California Christian Advocate, states that four gentlemen were living in the Valley at that time, having taken up "claims" there.

The first house was built in the Yosemite Valley in the autumn of 1856, opposite the Fall of that name: it is still standing, and is usually known as the Lower Hotel. At the locality a little over half a mile farther up the Valley a canvas house was built by G. A. Hite in the spring of 1857, and in the spring of the next year the present wooden house, now known as "Hutchings's Yosemite Hotel," was built by Hite and Beardsley. They kept it as a public house during that season, and it afterwards passed into the hands of Messrs. Sullivan and Cashman: it was next kept, in 1859–61, by Mr. Peck, then by Mr. Longhurst, and since 1864 by Mr. Hutchings. In the spring of 1857 Cunningham and Beardsley had a storehouse and shop just above the present Hutchings Hotel. The Lower Hotel was kept by John Reed in 1857, and by Mr. Cunningham from 1858 to 1861; it remained vacant for a couple of years, and was then taken by Mr. G. F. Leidig, who has kept it during the season of travel for the past three or four years.

Previous to 1864, the only actual settler and permanent resident in the Valley was Mr. J. C. Lamon, who took up his lonely quarters there in 1860. Many persons had been there during the summer, and numerous "claims" had been made, which were, of course, invalid under United States laws, as they were not accompanied by permanent residence, neither had the land ever been surveyed and brought into market, so that it was not open to pre-emption.

At the time that the Governor's proclamation was issued, taking possession of the Valley, and appointing Commissioners to protect and manage it, there were several residents and numerous claimants to various portions of the Valley and to "improvements" which had been made there. These claimants the Commissioners were disposed to treat, and to recommend to be treated by the State, with all possible consideration. They went to the extent of their powers by offering Messrs. Hutchings and Lamon leases for ten years of the premises occupied by them, at a nominal rent. This liberal offer these gentlemen saw fit to decline, believing that they could work upon public sympathy, and in some way influence the Legislature to grant them better terms, or perhaps even to look with favor on their pretensions to get possession of the Valley and hold it in fee simple. They appeared before the Legislature of 1867–68,—the next one to that which had accepted the Congressional grant,—and succeeded in procuring the passage of a bill giving them each 160 acres of land, and asking Congress to confirm this action. It is now stated, however, that, by some clerical oversight, this bill did not actually become a law. Be that as it may, this action of the Legislature of California came up in Congress for indorsement, and a bill or resolution to that effect did actually pass the House; but, reaching the Senate, was unfavorably reported on, and left on file for future action. What this action may be it is, of course, impossible to say; but what the result will be, if the bill passes, it will not be difficult to predict. The Yosemite Valley, instead of being held by the State for the benefit of the people, and "for public use, resort, and pleasure," as was solemnly promised, will become the property of private individuals, and will be held and managed for private benefit and not for the public good. As the tide of travel in the direction of this wonderful and unique locality increases, so will the vexations, restraints, and annoying charges, which are so universal at all places of great resort, be multiplied, and the Yosemite Valley, instead of being "a joy forever," will become, like Niagara Falls, a gigantic institution for fleecing the public. The screws will be put on just as fast as the public can be educated into bearing the pressure. Instead of having every convenience for circulation in and about the Valley, — free trails, roads, and bridges, with every facility offered for the enjoyment of Nature in the greatest of her works, unrestrained except by the requirements of decency and order, — the public will find, if the ownership of the Valley passes into private hands, that opportunity will be taken to levy toll at every point of view, on every trail, on every bridge, and at every turning, while there will be no inducement to do anything for the public accommodation, except that which may be made immediately available as a new means of raising a tax on the unfortunate traveller. Had the liberal policy inaugurated by the Legislature which accepted the grant (that of 1865-66) been carried out by its successor, — a policy which involved only a very small expenditure of money, — during the past season new trails and bridges would have been built, affording free access to every point of interest, and the present occupants of the Valley would have been in undisturbed possession of their premises, where they might remain so long as they were willing to conform to the few simple regulations of the Commissioners, forbidding wanton damage to the trees, shrubs, and flowers. Leases, on reasonable terms, would have been granted to such respectable parties as might apply for them, and multiplying facilities on every side would meet the increase of travel.

It has been argued that the Valley is large, and that the ceding of a couple of patches of only 160 acres each to private parties will have no seriously injurious consequences, — the bulk of the land would still remain in the hands of the Commissioners, to be managed for the benefit of the public. But there are only a little more than 1,100 acres of land in the Valley, within the rocky talus, or *débris* fallen from the walls, and of this only a small portion is valuable land for pasturage and cultivation, as well as desirable on account of its convenience of situation. Thus the holders of 320 acres of land judiciously selected would, in point of fact, have almost a monopoly of the Valley, especially as they would not be hampered by any restrictions, and would be above all control by the Commissioners. But, more than this, the whole Valley is already claimed, and if two of the claimants are to have their requests granted, the rest must be placed on the same footing; there would be neither justice nor reason in conceding 160 acres each to Messrs. Lamon and Hutchings, and not doing as much for others who made claims before either of these gentlemen. The whole Valley must be inevitably given up to the claimants, if any portion of it is; and the Commissioners would recommend that this should be done, in case Messrs. Lamon and Hutchings succeed in making good their pretensions. It would be entirely useless to attempt to exercise any useful control over the premises, with so large a portion of them withdrawn from supervision and placed in charge of irresponsible persons.

The State of California has, through its Legislature, assumed the responsibility and the guardianship of the grants of the Valley and the Big Tree Grove; she has solemnly promised to hold them "inalienable for all time." She has no right to attempt to withdraw from the responsibility she has voluntarily assumed. The equitable claims of the settlers in the Valley can be abundantly made good by a small amount of money, and it is astonishing that the great State of California should seek to avoid the performance of her agreement, — to repudiate her obligations, — merely to avoid the payment of the small sum which may be equitably due the parties who have been deprived, by the joint action of the State and of Congress, of their power to obtain, at some future time, a right in fee simple to the land they occupied. Legal rights these parties have not; the land had never been surveyed and opened to pre-emption. Their case is like that of thousands of others who have settled on the public land before it was surveyed, and who have afterwards been ousted by the General Government, when the ground they occupied was required for purposes of public good.

No: the Yosemite Valley is a unique and wonderful locality; it is an exceptional creation, and as such has been exceptionally provided for jointly by the Nation and the State,—it has been made a National public park and placed under the charge of the State of California. Let Californians beware how they make the name of their State a byword and reproach for all time, by trying to throw off and repudiate a noble task which they undertook to perform,—that of holding the Yosemite Valley as a place of public use, resort, and recreation, inalienable for all time!

CHAPTER II.

GENERAL.

THAT portion of the North American Continent which lies within the borders of the United States (leaving out of consideration the remote and isolated region now known as Alaska) presents to the traveller crossing it from east to west, in the pathway along which civilization has advanced, three well-marked grand divisions, which may be called the Eastern, Middle, and Western. On the East, we have the broad belt of the Appalachian chain of mountains, determining the general direction of the coast line, made up of a series of closely compacted wrinkles of the earth's crust, of no great elevation, never in its highest peaks quite reaching 7,000 feet, very uniform in direction and elevation over long distances, densely wooded, and offering in its fertile valleys and on its gently rising slopes every possible advantage of soil, forest, and water to benefit the settler. This series of ranges does not, however, rise at once from the edge of the Atlantic, but is prepared for, as it were, by a plain gently sloping upwards as we go west, and forming what is called the Atlantic Seaboard. This plain is about fifty miles wide in New England, where it is not so strongly marked a feature as farther south, in which direction it gains in width, extending as much as two hundred miles back from the sea in North and South Carolina. Leaving the seaboard, we rise among the Appalachian ranges, which form a belt of mountains averaging, perhaps, a hundred miles in width. Crossing this belt, and the broken foothill country which borders it on the west, forming the eastern side of Ohio, Kentucky, and Tennessee, we come in our western progress to the great central valley of the Continent, — the region drained by the Mississippi and the Missouri and their tributaries. At Pittsburg, the head of the Ohio proper, we are at an elevation of 699 feet above the sea-level; descending this river, we find ourselves, at its mouth and junction with the Mississippi, at 275 feet above the Gulf of Mexico, the average fall of the last-named river in that part of its course from the mouth of the Ohio to the Gulf being only three inches per mile. In following down the Ohio we are skirting the southern border of the region of prairies, the garden of the Continent, of which nearly the whole of Illinois may be taken as the type. Crossing the Mississippi, and still pursuing our westward course, we follow up the Missouri to the western line of the State of the same name, where the river bends to the north and leaves us the choice, if we wish to keep on directly west, of one of its great branches coming in from that direction, — the Platte and the Kansas. Up either of these we may travel for more than 500 miles, gradually and imperceptibly rising, an unbroken horizon in the distance, and a vast plain on either hand, absolutely destitute of trees, except along the banks of the streams, but abounding in nutritious grasses, the food of herds of buffaloes, once almost countless in numbers, but now rapidly disappearing before the rifle and the rail. These broad, almost endless seas of grazing-land are "the plains," not at all to be confounded with the "prairies." The plains form the western side of the great central valley, a region where, from climatological causes which cannot here be set forth, there is a great scarcity of rain, the amount of the annual precipitation diminishing rapidly as we go westward from the Mississippi River, until, between the 100th and 105th meridians it is no more than fifteen inches, or only one third of what it is near the meridian of 90°, in the centre of the great valley.

The edge of the great tangle of mountains which makes up the western third of our territory is encountered by the traveller coming from the east, after passing over a thousand miles in width of the central valley, in longitude 103°, if he strikes the Black Hills, in latitude 44°; or in 105°, if he follows up the Platte and finds himself at the base of the Rocky Mountains proper. From here west he will thread his way through narrow and intricate defiles, wind around or cross over innumerable spurs and ridges, traverse narrow valleys and occasional broad plains, the former sometimes green and attractive, the latter always arid and repulsive to the last degree; he will never descend below 4,000 feet above the sea-level, and will never be out of sight of mountains; these will always environ him, with thinly wooded flanks, and sterile and craggy summits, often glistening with great patches of snow, which gradually lessen as the summer advances. In the distance these mountain ranges, behind their atmosphere of purple haze, will seem massive and uniform in character; as he approaches each one, he will find it presenting some new charm of hidden valley or cañon deeply countersunk into the mountain side. As he rises still higher, he will quench his thirst at the refreshing spring of pure water fed by the melting snow above, while the grandeur of the rocky masses, the purity of the air, the solitariness and the almost infinite extent of the panorama opened before him, when he fairly reaches the summit, will leave upon his mind an ineffaceable impression of the peculiar features of our western mountain scenery. It is through and over these mountain ranges, passing north of Salt Lake, and striking the Humboldt River, which traverses the western side of the Great Basin at right-angles to the general direction of the chain, that the Pacific Railroad threads its way across the Continent.

This great mass of mountains, which fills the space between the 105th meridian and the Pacific Ocean so completely that it must be considered as a geographical unit, demands a distinct name by which it may be designated as a whole, as the geographer has every day occasion to do. The term "Rocky Mountains" has long been in use for a portion of its eastern border, and the "Sierra Nevada" and "Cascade Range" are equally well known appellations of the western edge of the great mass; while the almost innumerable broken and partially, but never quite, detached masses which fill up the interior receive their distinctive names as fast as they become known to the explorer or the settler. There is no name for the whole series of ranges, however; although in former days the term Rocky Mountains was more generally used than any other; but in the progress of exploration and geographical discovery this designation has become fully fixed on the group of ranges which surrounds the Parks in Colorado, Northern New Mexico, and Wyoming. Taken collectively, all the mountains bordering on the Pacific coast of America, from Cape Horn to the North Polar Sea, have been and still are by some geographers, designated as "*The Cordilleras*,"[*] a Spanish word signifying chains of mountains. The South American portion of the series was distinguished as the Cordilleras of the Andes, those of North America having no special designatory word corresponding to Andes, but being somewhat vaguely known as the Cordilleras of Mexico or of North America. As, in the progress of

---

[*] See Humboldt's "Aspects of Nature," English Edition, Vol. I. p. 56.

time, the name Andes has become firmly established in use as a general one for all the South American chains bordering the Pacific, without the additional word Cordilleras, I propose to use this exclusively for the North American chains, and, hereafter, to designate the great mass of mountains occupying the western side of the American Continent as THE CORDILLERAS, and trust that other geographers will see the propriety of the suggestion, and concur with me in adopting it. There is a greater propriety in using the word Cordilleras for the mass of North American mountains than for those of South America, for the latter are far more simple in their structure, being made up of a few great ranges, and not of a great number of smaller ones (Cordilleras) as on the northern division of the Continent.

The great region of the Cordilleras was pretty much a *terra incognita* only a quarter of a century ago. The explorations of Bonneville (1832 – 36) shed the first light on the region known as the Great Basin, and those of Fremont, a few years later (1842 – 45), made that generally known which had previously only been surmised, and laid a foundation, by an approximate determination of the latitude and longitude of a considerable number of important points, for a map of the central portion of the Cordilleras. Lewis and Clarke had previously (1805 – 7) made known the outlines of the geography of the country about the Upper Missouri and the Columbia Rivers, at the same time that Pike was exploring the head of the Arkansas River.

But little progress was made, however, towards anything like a reliable or complete map of the region west of the Rocky Mountains, until after the annexation of California to the United States and the discovery of gold in that region had given so prodigious an impetus to emigration to the Pacific coast, and led to a universal desire for railroad communication across the Continent, in place of the long and dangerous route by the Isthmus of Panama, or the tedious ride over the plains. The work of exploring a route for a Pacific railroad along several parallels of latitude, between Oregon on the north and Arizona on the south, was begun in 1853, and continued through that and the succeeding year by a considerable number of surveying parties, in charge of United States Engineer officers. The geographical results of these expeditions, with all the other material of this kind which could be collected from every possible source, were compiled into one general map by the United States Engineer Bureau, under the direction of Lieutenant (now

General) Warren. This map, which has been altered and corrected so many times at the Engineer Office, since its first appearance, in 1857, as to have become almost a new one, is the principal source from which compilers and publishers draw their material for maps of the Pacific States and Territories; but the study of it, by those familiar with the topography of portions of the region which it covers, will not fail to convince such persons that it can only be considered as a first rough sketch, nearly the whole of which must eventually give way to more reliable and accurate materials. The topographical work of the Central Pacific Railroad, done for the purpose of getting information for definitely locating its road, and the labors of the California Geological Survey, have already brought together a large amount of valuable material, which can be made available for improving the official map of the Engineer Bureau, and the results of the expedition now in the field under the direction of Mr. Clarence King will add still further of reliable information in regard to the geography of a considerable portion of the region in question.

The necessity of a good map of the Cordilleras will become more and more evident after the completion of the Pacific Railroad, which event will, no doubt, be followed by a great increase of travel, and especially of pleasure-travel, across the Continent. Four or five days from New York, or three from Chicago, will bring travellers into the high mountain region; and thousands who have already visited the Alps will seek for new impressions, and a new revelation of nature among the Cordilleras, rather than go over the old European ground a second or third time. Many English travellers for pleasure, among whom some, no doubt, of the renowned climbers of the Alpine Club will be found, will try their wind and muscle in a new field, and find health and excitement in climbing peaks which are yet unscaled, and in exploring regions where no foot of white man has ever been set. The inhabitants of the Mississippi Valley will seek refuge from the intense heat of summer among the lofty ranges of the no longer remote Pacific States; the invalid from the Eastern slope will exchange the cold, damp east wind for the invigorating mountain breeze, and will obtain a new lease of life while acquiring a knowledge of Nature's sublimest handiwork. For re-establishing the worn-out constitution, bracing up the shattered nerves, and bringing relief to the wearied soul, there is no panacea equal to mountain life and mountain scenery, taken in large doses, on the spot; and it is pleasant to think that we shall have the medicine at our own door hereafter, and not be obliged to cross the water in search of it. Besides, as a means of mental development, there is nothing which will compare with the study of Nature as manifested in her mountain handiwork. Nothing so refines the ideas, purifies the heart, and exalts the imagination of the dweller on the plains, as an occasional visit to the mountains. It is not good to dwell always among them, for "familiarity breeds contempt." The greatest peoples have not been those who lived on the mountains, but near them. One must carry something of culture to them, to receive all the benefits they can bestow in return.

But it is especially to California mountains and mountain scenery that this volume is dedicated, and to a small portion of these that it is to be more exclusively devoted, so that we must not tarry longer on the way to them.

Every one, be his acquaintance with the geography of our western border ever so slight, has at least some indistinct idea of the existence in California of two great masses of mountains, one called the Coast Ranges, the other the Sierra Nevada. The traveller, passing up the valley of the Sacramento or the San Joaquin, observes at a distance of twenty or thirty miles, on either hand, a continuous wall of mountains, which may appear in the dim distance, to the inexperienced eye, as a simple narrow uplift; both of these apparent walls are, in reality, broad belts of elevated ranges, the one averaging forty the other seventy miles in width, of which the detailed structure is exceedingly complicated, and whose grand dimensions can only be appreciated by those who have penetrated to their deepest recesses. On the east, we have the Sierra Nevada; on the west, the Coast Ranges, — the one not inaptly to be parallelized, in general extent and average elevation, with the Alps; the other but little inferior, in the same respects, to the Appalachian chain, — two grand features of the earth's surface which have for so many years occupied the attention of scientific observers and lovers of natural scenery. Of the eastern series of ranges, the most distant and loftiest elevations are never entirely bare of snow, and for a large portion of the year are extensively covered with it; the western ones, on the other hand, in the central portion of the State at least, have their highest peaks whitened for a few days only, during the coldest and stormiest winters. Hence the eastern heights were, long since, known to the Spaniards as the "Sierra Nevada," or "Snowy Range," Sierra being the almost exact equivalent of our word range, or mountain chain. The group of mountains on the western side and nearer the ocean naturally received the designation of "Coast Ranges" or Coast Mountains, the many subordinate ranges of which it is made up having received from the early Mexican-Spanish settlers the names of different saints, nearly exhausting the calendar.

The coast line of California, extending over ten degrees of latitude, or from near 32° to 42°, has a regular northwestern trend between the parallels of 35° and 40°, and the same regularity is found repeated in the interior features of the country between the same parallels. And, in order to bring vividly before the mind the grand simplicity of the topographical features of this part of the State, we may draw on the map five equidistant parallel lines, having a direction of N. 31° W., and 55 miles apart. Let the middle one of these be drawn at the western base of the Sierra Nevada; it will touch the edge of the foot-hills all along from Visalia to Red Bluff, a distance of nearly 400 miles. The first parallel east of this, drawn at 55 miles' distance, will pass through, or very near, the highest points of the Sierra Nevada from Mount Shasta on the north to Mount Whitney on the south. This line, running through the dominating peaks of the Sierra, and which is a very nearly straight one for 500 miles in length, we have called, in the California Geological Report, the main axial line of the State. Again, parallel to this on the east and at about the same constant distance of 55 miles from the summit of the Sierra, we find our line crossing a series of depressions, mostly occupied by lakes, which we may consider as representing the eastern base of the range. West of the great central valley, the fourth of our imaginary lines touches the eastern base of the Coast Ranges, and the fifth will approximately indicate the position of the edge of the Pacific, which is, of course, the western base of the same mountains.

This arrangement of lines indicates a division of the central portion of the State into four belts of nearly equal width, and which are indeed the best recognized features of its geography; they are known to all, mentioning them in their order from east to west, as the Eastern Slope, the Sierra, the Great Valley (or the Valley of the Sacramento and the San Joaquin,) and the Coast Ranges. The indicated arrangement holds good for a distance of 400 miles through the centre of the State, and through that portion of California which is by far the most important, both from an agricultural and mining point of view. Central California, as this division may properly be called, does not embrace over one third of the area of the State; but it holds at least 95 per cent of its population. The regions or divisions on each side of this central one are extremely mountainous and thinly inhabited. The southern portion is traversed by numerous broken ranges as yet but little explored, but characterized by extreme sterility, owing to the want of water, so that a large part can only be considered as an unmitigated desert. A narrow belt along the ocean, however, is more favored by climatic causes, and contains some tracts which are of unrivalled beauty and fertility. The northern division, again, is even more mountainous than the southern, portions of it being almost inaccessible. Along the coast and in much of the interior it is very heavily timbered; while, towards the eastern boundary of the State, it begins to exhibit the dryness and sterility characteristic of the Great Basin. It is a wild, rough region; and no small portion of it is pretty much given up to its aboriginal inhabitants, who have thus far held their own against the encroachments of the whites with pertinacity and no little success.

The Coast Ranges inosculate with the Sierra Nevada both north and south. In the neighborhood of the Tejon Pass, which is in about latitude 35°, the ridges of the two systems become topographically undistinguishable from each other; and it was only by careful examination of the position of the strata that we could discover where one system began and the other ended. So too, on the north, above Shasta City (latitude 40° 35'), the ranges close in on all sides, and to the traveller threading the innumerable cañons, there seems to be no clew to the labyrinth of chains, and no possibility of preserving the distinction between Coast Range and Sierra. But passing north into Oregon, we come, in latitude 44°, to the Willamette Valley, which here forms as marked a separation between the two systems of mountains as do the Sacramento or San Joaquin in California. Geologically, the Coast Ranges are made up of newer formations than the Sierra, and they have been subjected to great disturbances up to a very recent (geological) period. There are no rocks in the Coast Ranges older than the Cretaceous; strata of this and the Tertiary age making up nearly their whole body, with some masses of volcanic and granitic materials, neither, however, forming anything like a central nucleus or core.

The Coast Ranges do not exhibit any very lofty dominating peaks. The highest point in sight from San Francisco is Mount Hamilton, about fifteen miles east of San Jose; this is 4,440 feet high, or just 10,000 feet less than Mount Shasta. Still it does not rise conspicuously above the range in its vicinity, and it needs a sharp eye to pick it out at a little distance. Monte Diablo, although 584 feet lower (its elevation being 3,856 feet) is a much more conspicuous object, since it is quite isolated on the north side, owing to the great break in the range, which extends from the Golden Gate entirely across the chain. Indeed, the peculiar position of this mountain makes its graceful, double-pointed summit a very conspicuous landmark over a large portion of the State. North and south of the central portion, the Coast Ranges rise higher as they approach the Sierra in each direction, and the highest points attain as much as 8,000 feet.

The scenery of the Coast Ranges is rarely more than picturesque, but always peculiar, especially to those coming from the East. It is not so much the summits or ridges, as the valleys which nestle between them, and the remarkable vegetation of both valleys and slopes, which give character to the landscape. Besides, we must allow its share in producing the general impression to the peculiar erosion of the mountain masses, made conspicuous by the absence of forest vegetation, and, especially, to the peculiar atmosphere, which invests them with an indescribable charm.

The vegetation of these valleys and ranges is not remarkable for variety, for the number of forest trees exhibited is small; it is rather the distribution of the trees which makes them impressive. These are the most park-like valleys in the world. By far the largest number of trees in these valleys are oaks, and they grow, not uniformly distributed over the surface, but in graceful clumps, just as if arranged by the most skilful landscape gardener. The burr oak (*Quercus lobata*), is the one which gives, in the central Californian Valley, the most character to the landscape; it grows to a great size, and has the peculiar, gracefully-drooping branches of the American elm; some of the noblest specimens of it are to be found in Napa Valley. Other conspicuous oaks are the live oak (*Q. agrifolia*), a puzzle to botanists from the variability of its foliage, the white (*Q. Garryana*), the black (*Q. Sonomensis*) and the chestnut (*Q. densiflora*).

As we rise above the valleys, and especially in the vicinity of the ocean, and in the deep shaded cañons which intersect the mountains, and where the moisture brought by the winds from the sea is not too rapidly evaporated, we find a more considerable growth of forest-trees in the Coast Ranges, and especially as we proceed towards the northwest. Pines and oaks, however, everywhere greatly predominate. Of the pines, *Pinus Coulteri* is remarkable as having the largest and most beautiful cones of all the pines; *P. Sabiniana*, the digger pine, or silver pine, a very characteristic tree of the foot-hills, especially of the Sierra Nevada, up to 2,000 feet elevation, and also on the dry southerly hillsides of the Coast Ranges; *P. insignis*, the well-known ornamental "Monterey pine," quite limited in its distribution to some thousands of acres about Monterey and Carmelo; *P. muricata* is another Coast Range species, and *P. ponderosa* (the yellow pine) and *P. Lambertiana* (the sugar pine) are found in both Sierra and Coast Ranges. The redwood (*Sequoia sempervirens*) is also one of the grand characteristic trees of the Californian Coast Ranges, to which it is exclusively confined; with it grows frequently the well-known Douglas fir (*Abies Douglasii*). Besides these there are the laurel (*Tetranthera Californica*), of which the wood is now coming into use for ornamental cabinet work; the madrona,* a very characteristic and beautiful tree with its red bark and glossy leaves. The Monterey cypress (*Cupressus macrocarpa*) is another magnificent tree, greatly resembling the cedar of Lebanon; but strictly confined to one locality at Cypress Point, near Monterey. Of the shrubby undergrowth, the chamiso (*Adenostema fasciculata*), the manzanita (*Arctostaphylos glauca*), and different species of the *Ceanothus*, called "California lilac" by settlers from the Eastern States, on account of the resemblance of its perfume to that of the Eastern lilac, are the most prominent. These shrubs, separate or mingled together and associated with a variety of shrubby oaks, each furnished with as many thorns as there are points to leaves or branches, make what is universally known in California as "chaparral"; and large regions, especially near the summits of the mountains in the Coast Ranges, are often densely covered with this abominable undergrowth, utterly preventing free circulation, and rendering parts of the State quite inaccessible, — as, for instance, the mountains along the coast south of Monterey for a distance of a hundred miles, into whose recesses not even the explorer or the hunter has ever penetrated.

* Properly the "madroño," but everywhere called as written above.

There are many points of interest in the Coast Ranges which the tourist may visit; among them the Geysers, Clear and Borax Lakes, the New Almaden Mines, and, in general, all the valleys which connect with the Bay of San Francisco or are adjacent to it.* One gets a fine idea of the coast mountains and valleys by riding over the Santa Cruz Range to the town of that name; and a trip to the Geysers, coupled with the ascent of Sulphur (or Geyser) Peak, — a very easy climb from the stage road, — will show the traveller some of the most interesting features of the lower Californian ranges.

The most interesting short excursion, however, which can be made from San Francisco is the ascent of Monte Diablo, 3,856 feet high, and distant from the city, in a north-northeast direction, twenty-eight miles. The route to the foot of the mountain, which is usually ascended from the north side, is either by carriage or public conveyance from Oakland, by Walnut Creek and San Ramon Valley, to Clayton, at the base of the mountain; or, else, by steamboat to Benicia, ferry to Martinez, and carriage or stage to Clayton, via Pacheco. In either case Clayton is the point from which the ascent may be made, the distance to the summit being about six miles, and the excursion from Clayton and back being easily made, on foot or horseback, in a day, with time in the afternoon, if one should desire it, to return to Martinez the same night.† From the summit the view is panoramic, and perhaps unsurpassed in extent. Owing to the peculiar distribution of the mountain ranges of California, and the position of Monte Diablo in the centre of a great elliptic basin, the eye has full sweep over the slopes of the Sierra Nevada to its crest, from Lassen's Peak on the north to Mount Whitney on the south, a distance of fully 325 miles. It is only in the clearest weather that the details of the "Snowy Range" can be made out; but the nearer masses of the Coast Ranges, with their innumerable waves of mountains and wavelets of spurs, are visible, from Mount Hamilton and Mount Oso on the south to Mount Helena on the north. The great interior valley of California — the plains of the Sacramento and San Joaquin — are spread out under the observer's feet like a map, and they seem illimitable in extent.

* See "Map of the Vicinity of the Bay of San Francisco," published by the California Geological Survey, from which, at a glance, a better idea of the topography of the region may be obtained than could be given in a whole chapter of verbal description.

† There should be a good hotel at Clayton; if there were, no doubt pleasure travel to the mountain would be much increased.

The whole area thus embraced within the field of vision, as limited by the extreme points in the distance, is little less than 40,000 square miles, or almost as large as the whole State of New York. Mount Hamilton, fifteen miles east of San Jose, also commands a grand view, exclusively of the Coast Ranges; parties making a visit to this mountain, however, should be prepared to camp at its base, where there are all possible facilities of wood and water. The excursion from San Jose to the summit and back was made by our party in one day; but it is much better to take two for the trip, and it would not be easy to find a pleasanter camping-ground than presents itself on the banks of the Arroyo Hondo at the base of the mountain.

What gives its peculiar character to the Coast Range scenery is, the delicate and beautiful carving of their masses by the aqueous erosion of the soft material of which they are composed, and which is made conspicuous by the general absence of forest and shrubby vegetation, except in the cañons and along the crests of the ranges. The bareness of the slopes gives full play to the effects of light and shade caused by the varying and intricate contour of the surface. In the early spring these slopes are of the most vivid green, the awakening to life of the vegetation of this region beginning just when the hills and valleys of the Eastern States are most deeply covered by snow. Spring here, in fact, commences with the end of summer; winter there is none. Summer, blazing summer, tempered by the ocean fogs and ocean breezes, is followed by a long and delightful six months' spring, which in its turn passes almost instantaneously away, at the approach of another summer. As soon as the dry season sets in, the herbage withers under the sun's rays, except in the deep cañons, the surface becomes first of a pale green, then of a light straw-yellow, and finally, of a rich russet-brown color, against which the dark green foliage of the oaks and pines, unchanging during the summer, is deeply contrasted.

One need not go beyond the boundaries of the city of San Francisco to obtain fine panoramic views of Coast Range scenery; let the traveller, an hour before sunset, ascend Telegraph or Russian Hill of a clear day in the rainy season, — and such days are far from uncommon, — and he will have spread out before him the Golden Gate and the Bay of San Francisco, and the mountains which surround them, from Mount Bache and Mount Hamilton on the south to Mount Helena on the north. Looking in a northwesterly direction, he will see the ranges of Marin County coming down to meet the ocean, forming the northern side of the Golden Gate, and presenting at their termination a broken but precipitous wall of dark reddish rock, from six to eight hundred feet high, which contrasts finely with the rounded, green slopes above. Beyond these, the steep and graceful form of Tamal Pais is seen rising to the height of 2,597 feet, and forming the most prominent landmark of the region. This mountain lies six miles southwest of San Rafael, from which place the trip to its summit may easily be made on horseback in a day; and, although the view from it is not as extensive as that from Monte Diablo, it is one well worthy of being seen, as being both attractive and characteristic of the Coast Ranges, while the forest vegetation in the cañons on the north slope of the mountain is thoroughly Californian, consisting of noble specimens of the redwood, laurel, madrona, and other trees noticed above as occurring in this portion of the State. Facing the north, our observer from Telegraph Hill will have directly before him, at a distance of a mile, Alcatraz Island, with its fortifications, and beyond it, three miles farther on in the same direction, Angel Island, 771 feet high, intercepting the view up the bay of San Francisco and into San Pablo Bay, beyond which rise the numerous ranges which border Napa and Sonoma valleys, the farthest visible point in this direction being Mount Helena, 4,343 feet high, and about sixty miles distant. Facing the east, the view extends across the Bay, here about five miles wide, to the Contra Costa Hills, which rise rapidly from a gently sloping plain, two miles in width, to an average height of about 1,500 feet. Along the base of the Contra Costa Hills the population is rapidly increasing in density, — the towns of Oakland, San Antonio, Alameda, and San Leandro forming almost a continuous row of houses along a line some ten or twelve miles in length. Behind the Contra Costa Range rises the conical mass of Monte Diablo, apparently near at hand, but in reality belonging to a distant range, and separated from the Contra Costa Hills by the San Ramon Valley. To obtain, within the city itself, a clear view to the south, one must ascend the highest point of Clay Street Hill, or the elevation on which the reservoir is situated, just beyond Russian Hill; from these points the eye may range over the San Bruno Hills, down the bay into the San Jose Valley, and as far as the great mass of mountains near and west of Mount Hamilton and Mount Oso, — a wild waste of chaparral-covered ridges, into which few persons have ever penetrated. This portion of the Coast Ranges sometimes remains covered with snow for days, or, during exceptionally cold and stormy winters, weeks even, and at such times presents an almost Alpine appearance. On the other side of the San Jose Valley we look along the hills covered with redwood forests — now, alas! fast disappearing before the chopper's axe — as far as Mounts Bache, Chual, and Umunhum, which rise directly above the village and mines of New Almaden, the highest of these, named in honor of the late eminent chief of the Coast Survey, being just sixty feet lower than Monte Diablo. From some points between the city and the ocean, in certain states of the atmosphere, the Farallones are distinctly visible, forty miles out at sea, their precipitous granite masses gleaming white in the sun.

But we linger too long among the Coast Ranges, and must turn to the grander Sierra, in which the localities more particularly the theme of this volume are situated.

The Sierra Nevada, or "Snowy Range," forms the western edge of the great continental upheaval or plateau, on which the Cordilleras are built up. It corresponds in position to the Rocky Mountains, the one being the western, the other the eastern edge of the central portion of the mass. The base of the Rocky Mountains, however, is 4,000 feet above the sea level, and the slope from it eastward is almost imperceptible, but continuous for 600 miles to the Mississippi; while from the crest of the Sierra Nevada we descend rapidly, in less than a hundred miles, to very near the level of the sea. The plateau between the two ranges is nearly a thousand miles wide, having here its greatest development and its maximum altitude, while the subordinate ranges piled upon it here exhibit their greatest regularity of trend and structure.

No range among all the mountain chains which make up the Cordilleras of North America surpasses, if any one equals, the Sierra Nevada, in extent or altitude, and certainly no one on the continent can be compared with it in the general features of interest which characterize it, — its scenery, vegetation, mineral wealth, the energy and skill with which its resources have been developed, and the impetus which this development has given to commerce and civilization.

The Sierra Nevada, as the term is popularly understood, is strictly limited to California, and it extends from the Tejon Pass to Mount Shasta, a distance of over 550 miles. Some, however, and with propriety, would consider the Sierra as terminating at Lassen's Peak, a grand volcanic mass in latitude 40° 30′, where the metamorphic rocks of the Sierra system sink down in a great transverse break, and a volcanic plateau takes their place and stretches north to Mount Shasta. Beyond this last-named volcanic mass, the range is prolonged to the north through Oregon and Washington Territory, with much the same character as in California, although with greatly diminished average elevation; but it is there everywhere known by the name of the Cascade Range. In its southern termination, as previously remarked, the Sierra Nevada inosculates with the Coast Ranges, and the two systems are so linked together from the Tejon Pass south, that there is no longer any geographical, but only a geological, distinction to be made between the two systems.

Considering the Sierra to terminate on the north at Lassen's Peak, its length will be about 450 miles, and its breadth, taking the valleys of Walker's, Mono, and Honey Lakes as its eastern, and the base of the foot-hills as its western limit, may be set down as averaging 80 miles. This width, however, is very unequally distributed between the two slopes: the western is much more gradual, and of course longer, especially as the elevation to be gained is much greater; for the western descent is to the level of the sea, or nearly to that; while the eastern is to the level of the Great Basin, some 4,000 feet above tide-water. The western slope of the Sierra rises, in the central portion of the State, opposite Sacramento, at the average rate of about 100 feet to a mile, the elevation of the passes being about 7,000 feet, and the horizontal distance seventy miles. As we go south from here the elevation of the passes increases rapidly and the breadth of the range diminishes, until the grade reaches its maximum opposite Visalia, where the average rise from the plain of the San Joaquin to the summit of the passes is over 240 feet to the mile, and to the summit of the highest peaks 300 feet. North of the Donner Lake Pass, or that by which the Central Pacific Railroad crosses the Sierra, the branches of the Feather River head around and to the east of an elevated range on which Spanish Peak and Lassen's Peak are situated, while the real divide or water-shed is forty miles farther east, and crowned with numerous peaks, few of which are named and none known to geographers. The intermediate space between these two dominating ranges is filled with a labyrinth of ridges and valleys, defying all attempts at classification. The average slope from Oroville to the summit of Beckworth's Pass is not over seventy feet to the mile; but, owing to the peculiar character of the country indicated above, this more moderate elevation and grade could not be made available for railroad purposes, as the summit could not be reached, except by a circuitous and difficult route up one of the branches of the Feather River.

The height of the dominating peaks, as well as of the passes, sinks as we go northward from latitude 36° 30′, which is nearly that of the north end of Owen's Lake. This condition of things will be easily understood on examination of the annexed tabular statement:--

TABLE OF THE ELEVATIONS OF PEAKS AND PASSES IN THE SIERRA NEVADA.

Latitude.		Name and Elevation of Pass.		Name and Elevation of Adjacent Dominating Peak.	
°	′		No. of Feet.		No. of Feet.
36	32	Pass without name	12,057	Mount Whitney	15,000
37	28	" " "	12,400	Red Slate Peak	13,400
37	55	Mono Pass	10,765	Mount Dana	13,227
38	10	Sonora Pass	10,115	Castle Peak	12,500
38	30	Silver Mountain Pass	8,793	Silver Mountain	10,934
38	45	Carson Pass	8,759	Wood's Peak	10,552
38	50	Johnson Pass	7,339	Pyramid Peak	10,120
39	10	Georgetown, or Squaw Valley Pass	7,119	No very marked dominating peaks; the crest of the range from 500 to 1,000 feet above the passes.	
39	20	Donner Pass	7,056		
39	30	Henness Pass	6,996		
39	38	Yuba Gap	6,642	Downieville Buttes	8,400
39	45	Beckworth's Pass	5,327	Onjumi	8,378

From Beckworth's north, the passes gain a little in elevation, and the adjacent peaks are from 8,000 to 9,000 feet high. The above table shows that from latitude 36° 32′ to 39° 45′ the peaks sink from 15,000 to 8,400, and the passes from 12,000 to 5,400 feet.

The central mass, or core, of the Sierra Nevada, as of most high mountains, is chiefly granite; this is flanked on both sides by metamorphic slates, and capped irregularly by vast masses of basaltic and other kinds of lava, and heavy beds of ashes and breccia, bearing witness to a former prodigious activity of the subterranean volcanic forces, now dormant or only made sensible by occasional earthquake shocks. The granitic belt widens as we go south, and, in the highest portion of the Sierra, has a breadth of nearly forty miles. Northwards, the amount of volcanic material increases, and, after we pass Lassen's Peak, as before remarked, it covers the whole width of the range, forming one vast elevated plateau, crowned with a series of cones, many of which have well-formed craters still existing on their summits. These craters, however, now exhibit no indications of present activity. The only remnants of the forces by which they were built up are the hot springs, which are plentifully distributed along the line of former volcanic action. While the southern highest points of the Sierra are of granite, and those north of Lake Tahoe are chiefly volcanic, or, at least, capped with volcanic materials, there are a number of very elevated peaks in the central part of the State, including Mount Dana, which are made up of slates and metamorphic rocks, as will be noticed in the next chapter.

In so elevated a range as the Sierra Nevada, we should expect to find a number of belts of forest vegetation, corresponding to the different zones of altitude above the sea-level. As in the Coast Ranges, the general character is given to the landscape by coniferous trees and oaks, all other families being usually quite subordinate in importance, and the number of the conifers, as compared with that of the oaks, increasing rapidly as we ascend.

There are four pretty well marked belts of forest vegetation on the west slope of the Sierra, and that of the eastern slope would make a fifth for the whole range. These belts, however, pass gradually into each other, and are not so defined that lines can be drawn separating or distinctly limiting them, and the division into groups or belts here proposed will only be found to hold good in the central portion of the State; as we go north, all the groups of species gradually descend in elevation, especially in approaching the coast.

Of the four belts on the western slope of the Sierra the lowest is that of the foot-hills, extending up to about 3,000 feet in elevation; its most characteristic species are the digger pine (*P. Sabiniana*) and the black oak (*Q. Sonomensis*); these stand sparsely scattered over the hillsides, or in graceful groups, nowhere forming what can be called a forest. The pale bluish tint of the pine leaves contrasts finely with the dark green of the oak foliage, and both pines and oaks are strongly relieved, in summer, against the amber and straw-colored ground. The small side valleys, gulches or cañons, as they are called in California, according to their dimensions, are lined with flowering shrubs, of which the California "buck-eye" (*Æsculus Californica*), is, at this altitude, by far the most conspicuous, gradually giving place, as we ascend, to the various species of the delightfully fragrant *Ceanothus*, or California lilac. Manzanita and chamiso are, of course, abundant everywhere, and especially on the driest hillsides and summits.

The next belt is that of the pitch pine, or *Pinus ponderosa*, the sugar pine (*P. Lambertiana*), the white or bastard cedar (*Libocedrus decurrens*), and the Douglas spruce (*Abies Douglasii*); this is peculiarly the forest belt of the Sierra Nevada, or that in which the trees have their finest development. The pitch pine replaces the digger pine first, and more and more of the sugar pine is seen from about 4,000 feet on to 5,000, at which altitude the last-named noble and peculiarly Californian tree is most abundant. The sugar pine is remarkable for the size of its cones, which hang in bunches of two or more from the ends of the long branches, like ornamental tassels. The timber of this tree is the best that California furnishes, and its size gigantic, being not unfrequently 300 feet in height and from seven to ten feet in diameter. It is also in this belt that the "Big Trees" belong.

The third zone of forest vegetation is that of the firs (*Picea grandis* and *amabilis*), with the tamarack pine (*P. contorta*) taking to a considerable extent the place of the pitch and sugar pines. This belt extends from 7,000 to 9,000 feet above the sea, in the central part of the State. The traveller to the Yosemite will see it well developed about Westfall's meadows and from there to the edge of the Valley. These firs, especially the *amabilis*, which is distinguished by the geometrical regularity with which its branches are divided, are most superb trees; they attain a large size, are very symmetrical in their growth, and have a dark green brilliant foliage, which is very fragrant. A pine called *Pinus Jeffreyi*, by some considered a variety of the *ponderosa*, is also a characteristic tree of the upper part of this belt, and above this sets in the *Pinus monticola*, which takes the place of the *Piceas* at a high elevation.

The highest belt of all is that of the *Pinus albicaulis* (or *flexilis* of some botanists), which marks the limit of vegetation in the middle and northern Sierra, *Pinus aristata* taking its place in the more southern region about the head of King's and Kern Rivers. The *albicaulis* generally shows itself at the line just where vegetation is going to give out altogether, as around the base of Mount Clark, Mount Dana, and Mount Shasta. On the last-named mountain it was seen growing, as a shrub, in favorable places, up to 9,000 feet; and small trees were so compacted by the pressure of the snow on them in the winter, that a man could easily walk over the flat surface formed by their foliage. A little clump of this species just at the edge of the snow, on Lassen's Peak, shows the aspiring character of this tree, which is one widely distributed over the high mountain-tops of the Cordilleras. The *aristata* is also found in the Rocky Mountains, as well as along a limited part of the highest region of the Sierra Nevada.

More details of the distribution of the forest trees in and about the Yosemite will be found in the two following chapters; the above very general and brief remarks seemed necessary to our hasty sketch of the general features of the Sierra Nevada.

The climate of the Sierra Nevada varies, of course, with the altitude; but not so much, nor so rapidly, as one would expect. Indeed, the traveller, leaving San Francisco, will have to rise several thousand feet on the flanks of the Sierra, before he will come to a region where the mean temperature of summer is as low as in that city. As high up as 8,000 or 10,000 feet, even, the days are quite comfortably warm. On the very highest peaks, at elevations of 12,000 or 13,000 feet, we rarely felt the want of an overcoat at midday. An examination of our thermometrical observations shows that we had the mercury almost always over 80° in the Yosemite Valley, at an elevation of 4,000 feet above the sea, during the six midday hours, in June and July, although the nights were, almost without exception, cool enough to make a pair of heavy blankets desirable. At our camp in the Tuolumne Valley, during the same months, at an elevation of 8,700 feet, the mercury stood at a little over 60°, usually, during the hours from 11 to 3, but fell rapidly after sunset; and, in one case, solid ice an inch thick was formed during the night. At the summit of Mount Dana, 13,227 feet high, the temperature marked at noon was 43°; and on Red Mountain, at an elevation of nearly 12,000 feet, the thermometer stood at 58°. At high altitudes, all through the mountains, the weather during the summer is almost always the finest possible for travelling, whether for scientific purposes or for pleasure. The nights, indeed, are cold; but fuel is abundant, and the system becomes braced up to endure what, in lower regions, would seem unbearable. There are occasional storms in the high mountains; but, in ordinary seasons, these are quite rare, and one of the greatest drawbacks to the pleasure of travelling in the Alps, the uncertainty of the weather, is here almost entirely wanting. One may be reasonably sure, in starting to climb a mountain peak, of a clear sky, and a temperature which will make walking and riding a pleasure.

In the mountains there is almost always a breeze during the day; but this rarely in summer rises to a gale. In the daytime the air draws up the mountain slopes, and in the night blows down. Hence travellers always have the dust with them, in ascending, until they get above roads and wheeled vehicles,—a great annoyance, and a serious drawback to the pleasure of travelling, the only compensation for which is to be found in the fact that, in going down the mountains and towards the Bay of San Francisco, whether approaching it from north or south, you have the breeze in your face and the dust behind you.

The high mountains of California receive, probably, their whole precipitation of moisture in the form of snow, and of this an enormous amount falls, and during the winter months almost exclusively. In the central portion of the State snow is not frequent, neither does it lie long on the ground, at localities below 3,000 feet in altitude. As we go higher than this, the snow-fall increases rapidly, and it accumulates in immense bodies on the mountain slopes, and especially in the cañons. Nearly one hundred inches of rain fell in the Sierra, during the stormy winter of 1867–68, along a belt 2,000 feet above the sea-level, and we can easily believe the statement that over sixty feet of snow fell during that season at Donner Lake, not quite 6,000 feet in altitude. The variation in the fall of rain or snow, from winter to winter, is very great all through California. During ordinary years, however, the flanks of the Sierra are well covered down to 4,000 feet above the sea, during the midwinter months, and a heavy body of snow lies on the passes until May, or even June.

The crest of the Sierra is never entirely denuded of its snow; although at the end of a long and dry summer, following an unusually dry winter, there are no heavy bodies of it except in the cañons, on the northern slopes of the very highest peaks. There is ordinarily but little if any snow left, at the end of the summer, along the crest of the mountains between Henness

Pass and Lassen's Peak. One or two of the other highest points in Plumas County showed, here and there, a spot of snow, on their northern slopes, in 1866, until nearly the end of the summer; but on Lassen's Peak quite large bodies of snow remain permanently, as far down as 2,000 feet below the summit. From here north to Mount Shasta there is no lasting accumulation of snow; but on that peak there are always, throughout the season, great masses in the ravines or cañons on all sides, extending down to 6,000 or 7,000 feet below the summit. It is here, and here only, that a pretty well defined "line of perpetual snow" may be said to exist. Seen from a great distance, Mount Shasta appears as a dazzlingly white cone of snow; but, from a point only a few miles off, it is evident enough that the ridges and crests between the ravines furrowing its sides are bare, and that these form a large portion of the whole surface.

It is the melting in summer of the snow accumulated during the winter which keeps the streams full of water, high up in the mountains, and these, in turn, furnish the canals or ditches which convey the indispensable supply to the miners. These ditches are deep in proportion to their width, and have a rapid fall, so as to lessen the evaporation, which so rapidly diminishes the quantity of water in the streams flowing naturally down the Sierra, the smaller of which usually become quite dry before the summer is half over. Thus the store of snow laid by in the Sierra is a most precious treasure to the State; for, if all the precipitation were in the form of rain, it would run off at once, causing devastating floods, and in the summer it would be impossible to carry on agricultural or mining operations. Indeed, without the supply of snow, the whole country would become a perfect desert. All through the Great Basin it is the melting of the winter's stock of snow which gives what little there is of verdure and fertility to the slopes of the mountains. When the ranges are lofty enough and wide enough to collect and store away a large supply, which as it melts will furnish water to irrigate the slopes and valleys, these may be made to bear abundant crops; where, on the other hand, the ridges are low, they, as well as the valleys at their bases, are absolutely sterile.

The snow seems to disappear from the summits of the higher peaks by evaporation, rather than by actual melting. On the top of Mount Shasta, for instance, there was no indication of dampness; indeed, pieces of paper, with the names of visitors written on them, and laid in uncorked bottles, or on the rocks themselves, were found by us to have remained for years as fresh and free from mould or discoloration as when first left there. It is owing to this peculiar dryness of the air, probably, that there are no indications of the present existence of glaciers on Mount Shasta; and, if not occurring there, they could not be expected to be found anywhere else in California. Masses of snow several miles long, and hundreds of feet in thickness, remain all summer without showing any indication of becoming glacier ice. They freeze and thaw on the surface, and gradually waste away, without giving rise to considerable streams, remaining always snow and nothing but snow.

At a former and not very remote geological period, however, there were immense glaciers in the Sierra Nevada, and the traces of their past existence are among the most interesting phenomena to be observed there now. The same beautifully striated and polished surfaces of rock, resulting from the pressure and sliding of great masses of ice over them, — the same peculiar accumulations of gravel and boulders, called "moraines" in the Alps, and which are always formed where glaciers exist, are found in the Sierra over a great extent of surface. These manifestations of former glacial agencies are limited to the higher part of the range, and are most abundant and well-defined about the heads of Kern and King's Rivers, in the region above the Yosemite, and in the valleys in which the Merced, San Joaquin, and Tuolumne head, as will be more fully noticed in a succeeding chapter. The facts observed prove clearly that the climate of California was once considerably moister than it now is. There must have been a pretty abundant precipitation of snow along the Sierra, during the summer, as there now is in the Alps; but it is not necessary to suppose that the country, at the base of the mountains at least, was uninhabitable. The glaciers did not extend, in the central portion of the State, down below 6,000 to 8,000 feet above the sea-level, except in a few exceptional localities. In these, the configuration of the mountain valleys at the head of the glaciers was such as to give occasion for the accumulation of exceptionally great masses of snow. Such cirques, or amphitheatres, exist now at the heads of the largest Alpine glaciers. Of these former low-descending ice-masses in California, one of the most striking was that which came down the valley of the Tuolumne, and which must have been over thirty miles in length.

That there was formerly a much greater precipitation of moisture on the eastern side of the Sierra than there now is, seems proved by the former greater extension of the lakes on the eastern slope. Mono Lake, for instance, is surrounded by terraces or benches, which show that its surface once stood 600 feet higher than it now does, and the same is true of Walker, Pyramid, and the other lakes on that side of the Sierra. No doubt, at that time, the now arid valleys of Nevada were beautiful inland seas, which filled the spaces between the lofty parallel ridges by which that State is traversed. Perhaps the slopes of those ridges were then clothed with dense forests, offering a wonderful contrast to the present barrenness of the ranges, and the monotony and desolation of the alkaline plains at their bases.

CHAPTER III.

THE YOSEMITE VALLEY.

THE Yosemite Valley is situated a little south of east from San Francisco, and is distant from that city about 155 miles in a direct line; but by either of the routes usually travelled it is nearly 250, as will be seen from the annexed tables, which give the estimated distances of the Valley from Stockton, by each of the three routes which it is possible to take by the ordinary public conveyances. Stockton itself, usually called 120 miles by water from San Francisco, is now reached by steamboat from the city in about twelve hours. Boats leave San Francisco at four o'clock P. M., and arrive at Stockton early the next morning, in ample time to connect with the stages which leave the last-named place for various points in the mountains at six o'clock A. M. A railroad between the two cities will probably soon make some changes in the time of leaving both.

From Stockton there are, nominally, three routes to the Yosemite; but, of late, almost all the travel has been by two of them, the third, that by Big Oak Flat, being almost entirely neglected. Yet this is the most direct line to the Valley, passengers by either of the other routes making a considerable detour to the south. A straight line from Stockton to the Yosemite passes directly through Big Oak Flat, and the distance is only ninety miles in an air-line.

A railroad has also been talked of for some time between Stockton and Copperopolis. This would shorten the time to the Yosemite considerably, and perhaps bring the Big Oak Flat route into fashion. Those who can afford it will do well to hire private conveyances at Stockton, as the stages are often crowded and uncomfortable, the arrangements on the route not having been hitherto made with reference to the comfort of pleasure travellers.

The tables of distances from Stockton, by the different routes, are as follows:—

VIA BIG OAK FLAT.

		Miles.	
By stage or other wheeled vehicle.	Stockton to Copperopolis	36	
	Copperopolis to Chinese Camp	15	
	Chinese Camp to Jacksonville	4	
	Jacksonville to Big Oak Flat	8	63
On horseback.	Big Oak Flat to Sprague's Ranch	9	
	Sprague's Ranch to Big Flume	4	
	Big Flume to South Fork, Tuolumne River	3	
	South Fork to Hardin's Ranch	4	
	Hardin's Ranch to Tamarack Flat	14	
	Tamarack Flat to Boundary Corner, Yosemite	2¾	
	Boundary Corner to Lower Hotel	7½	44¼
	Total		107¼

VIA COULTERVILLE.

		Miles.	
By stage.	Stockton to Knight's Ferry	36	
	Knight's Ferry to Crimea House	12	
	Crimea House to Don Pedro's Bar	9	
	Don Pedro's Bar to Coulterville	14	71
Horseback or on wheels.	Coulterville to Bower Cave	12	
	Bower Cave to Black's	5	
On horseback.	Black's to Deer Flat	6	
	Deer Flat to Hazle Green	5½	
	Hazle Green to Crane Flat	5	
	Crane Flat to Tamarack Flat	4¾	
	Tamarack Flat to Boundary	2¾	
	Boundary Stake to Edge of Valley	0½	
	Edge of Valley to Lower Hotel	7	48½
	Total		119½

VIA BEAR VALLEY AND MARIPOSA.

		Miles.	
By stage or on wheels.	Stockton to Tuolumne River	45	
	Tuolumne River to Snelling's	12	
	Snelling's to Hornitos	12	
	Hornitos to Bear Valley	9	
	Bear Valley to Mariposa	12	
	Mariposa to White and Hatch's	11¾	101¾
On horseback.	White and Hatch's to Clark's	11⅝	
	Clark's to Alder Creek	6½	
	Alder Creek to Empire Camp	3	
	Empire Camp to Westfall's Meadow	3½	
	Westfall's Meadow to Inspiration Point	5	
	Inspiration Point to Lower Hotel	7½	37⅛
	Total		138⅞

Thus it will be seen that the distances to be travelled by the different routes are as follows:—

	B. O. Flat.	Coulterville.	Mariposa.
On wheels	63	71	101¾ miles.
Horseback	44¼	48½	37¼ "
Total	107¼	119½	138⅞

And, having given the distances, as above, we will add a few words as to the desirability of the different routes. In the first place, it must be mentioned that the roads into the Valley all have a great fault; the traveller is obliged to rise from 3,000 to 3,500 feet higher than the point which he wishes to reach, namely, the bottom of the Yosemite Valley, which is only 4,000 feet above the sea-level, while the highest point on the Mariposa trail is 7,400 feet in elevation, and the summit on the Coulterville and Big Oak Flat side not much less. The reason of this is, that the cañon of the Merced, which river runs through the Valley, is deep and crooked, and has such precipitous sides, that making a road or trail through it would be quite difficult and expensive, so that the Valley has to be approached, not from below, but from one side. Still, the Indians have a trail on the south side of the Merced, from Clark's ranch, which is used by them when the other is closed by snow, and which we suppose to be at least 2,000 feet lower than the other, and which consequently is open earlier in the spring and closed later in the autumn. If a good trail could be made into the Valley this way, not only would the extra climbing and descending be avoided, but, what is of more importance, the Valley would be accessible to travellers, not liking to go in over the snow, for a much longer time during the season. At present there is sometimes a considerable amount of snow to be crossed in going in, on either side, as late as June, although, generally, the trail is clear in May.

It is usually a great desideratum with travellers to shorten the distance to be made on horseback as much as possible, and in this respect it will be seen that the Mariposa trail has the advantage, as there are only 37 miles of horseback riding on that side to 48 on the other. With a little expense, however, the trail on the Coulterville side may easily be shortened so that it shall not be much longer than the other. This may be done by making a straight road from the Bower Cave to Deer Flat, by which five or six miles may be saved, as will be seen on the map. A good wagon-road can be made on this side from Coulterville to the edge of the Valley, for a very moderate sum, so that travellers could make the trip through in one day; indeed, there is now a wagon-road as far as Black's, although it is seldom used. As at present arranged, it is very inconvenient to travellers, especially to ladies not accustomed to riding, since there is no stopping-place on that side, except at Black's (which is an excellent one); but this being only seventeen miles from Coulterville, there are 31½ miles to be done the next day, — a very hard day's work, when we consider that climbing down the walls of the Valley makes up a part of it.

The proper way for travellers is, undoubtedly, to make the "round trip," going into the Valley on one side and returning on the other, as the trail on the Mariposa side takes one near the Big Trees, and, besides, furnishes by far the best general views of the Valley; while, on the Coulterville trail, we have the Bower Cave and many fine views of the distant Sierra. It is for the traveller to decide whether he prefers getting these general views of the Valley after he has already been there, or on his way into it. If he wishes to have the whole grandeur of the Yosemite revealed to him at once, let him enter the Valley on the Mariposa side; if, on the other hand, he prefers to see the various points in succession, one after another, and then, finally, as he leaves the Valley, to have these glorious general views, as a kind of summing up of the whole, he will enter by the Coulterville and depart by the Mariposa side. Horses and guides may be obtained at Coulterville, Mariposa or Bear Valley, to make the round trip, and parties often go prepared to camp out on the way wherever they may find it agreeable, thus rendering themselves independent of hotels and landlords. Those who do not camp usually ride from Bear Valley or Mariposa to White and Hatch's, dine there, and go on to Clark's the same evening; stop over there one day, and visit the Big Tree Grove; then ride to the Yosemite the next day. In leaving the Valley, they ride to Black's the first day; then to Coulterville the second, and reach San Francisco late the night of the third. Those who are not in haste should stop over night at White and Hatch's, and jog on comfortably the next day to Clark's. Persons have been found, sufficiently in haste, and having so little regard for their horses, as to ride from Bear Valley to the Yosemite in one day, eighteen hours long!

With the completion of the railroad from San Francisco to Stockton, and from the latter place to Copperopolis, as well as of the wagon-roads contemplated and spoken of above, the trip to the Yosemite will no longer be one requiring any considerable exertion, even from those least used to "roughing it." As at present arranged, however, it will not do to take less than ten days for the excursion from San Francisco to the Yosemite and back, including a visit to the Big Trees. This includes a stoppage of three days in the Valley, — the least time that one can give to it, even if all the minor excursions are neglected. The following would be a convenient programme: leave on Stockton boat at four o'clock P. M.; then *first* day to Bear Valley; *second*, to White and Hatch's; *third*, visit the Big Trees and return to Clark's; *fourth*, to the Yosemite; *fifth*, *sixth*, and *seventh*, in the Valley; *eighth*, to Black's; *ninth*, to Bower Cave and Coulterville; *tenth*, return to San Francisco, leaving Coulterville very early in the morning and reaching San Francisco late the same night. There is nothing in the trip which need excite alarm in even the most timid person, as the trails are nowhere dangerous, and it is always easy to dismount where the slope is too steep for riding with comfort to man or beast. The grandeur of the scenery, the magnificence of the forests, the clear cool water, and bracing air of the mountains, — all these combine to make the ride, after one leaves the foot-hills, one of most intense enjoyment to those who are sufficiently accustomed to riding to feel "at home" on a horse's or mule's back, as is usually the case with Californians. Three days, however, is but a very limited time for seeing the Valley itself and its surroundings; and, after describing the principal objects of interest in the region, some hints will be given as to extending the sojourn there and utilizing the additional days to the best advantage.

For convenience, the routes into the Valley, on each side, will first be described, and then the Valley itself, and we will imagine the traveller to start at Coulterville, entering the Yosemite on the north side.

Coulterville lies near the "Great Quartz Vein" of California, and was once the seat of considerable placer and quartz mining; but both of these industries are, at present, in rather a stagnant condition. It lies on Maxwell Creek, a branch of the Merced, at an elevation of about 1,800 feet above the sea, and not far from the border between the "foot-hills" and the Sierra proper, where we leave the hills densely covered with chaparral for the more open and majestic forests of the higher regions, exchanging ditches for naturally-running water, no longer thickened to the consistency of porridge by the red mud of the miner. The road runs from Coulterville nearly northeast for eight miles, until it strikes the North Fork of the Merced, down which it descends for a short distance, then crosses and passes near the "Bower Cave." This is a picturesque and quite unique locality, and is well worthy of a visit.

It consists of an immense crack in the limestone, open to the air at the surface, and irregularly widened out in a cave-like manner below, by the action of currents of water. On the upper side of the obliquely-descending crevice, an overhanging ledge of rock permits the vertical depth of the cave to the level of the water, which partly fills it, to be measured; it is 109 feet. The length of the open crevice is 133 feet, and its width 86. At various heights, deep cavities, or small caves, are worn in the rock, some of which may be followed for a considerable distance. The picturesque effect of the cave is greatly heightened by the growth within it of three large maple trees, of which the branches project out at the top. The water at the bottom is exceedingly pellucid, permitting the ramifications of the crevice beneath its surface to be seen for a depth of at least forty feet. Access can be had to the bottom of the cave by a series of steps, and a boat is provided for the use of visitors; other conveniences are also furnished, permitting a cool and comfortable stay in this curious place, which seems to be peculiarly adapted for a picnic in hot weather.

From the Bower Cave, the road follows down the north fork of the Merced for three miles, then crosses over rolling hills to Black's, about the same distance farther. Here the first night is usually spent, the accommodations being excellent. From Black's, the trail winds along the side of the narrow valley of Bull Creek, completely embowered in ceanothus, or California lilac, most fragrant during the early part of the season. Leaving Bull Creek, we follow Deer Creek, one of its branches, to its source at Deer Flat. This is one of the numerous small, nearly level, areas of grassy land, usually called "flats" in the Sierra. Here was formerly, and perhaps is still, the last habitation on the trail, and good camping ground, although rather wet early in the season.

Leaving Deer Flat, the trail winds up along the side of Pilot Peak, a prominent landmark, a little over 6,000 feet above the sea-level, the summit of which may be easily reached from the trail, and the view from which will well repay a delay of a couple of hours for that purpose. There are few points of easy access finer than Pilot Peak for a general view of the Sierra, the crest of which is about forty miles distant in a straight line. In clear weather, in spite of this distance, an admirable panoramic view may be obtained, especially of the almost inaccessible volcanic region south of the Sonora trail, where Castle Peak, one of the grandest mountain masses in California, rises in steps like a series of truncated pyramids piled one above the other. This point is twenty-five miles distant in a northeasterly direction. Sweeping round the horizon, to the right from Castle Peak, we see, beyond the Yosemite, the highest portion of the Sierra, at the head of the Merced River, a magnificent group of peaks over 13,000 feet in elevation. The summit of Pilot Peak is also an excellent point for getting an idea of the middle portion of the Sierra Nevada, the region of deep cañons and innumerable, long, parallel ridges, all clad with dense forests of coniferous trees.

From Deer Flat to Crane Flat is ten and a half miles (usually called twelve), Hazle Green being midway between the two; these are all small patches of meadow. The trail passes over and along a high granite spur of the Sierra, rising at the summit to the elevation of 6,669 feet. From this portion of the route there are occasional glimpses to be had of the crest of the Sierra, especially from a ridge a few rods to the south of the trail, at a point two miles beyond Hazle Green. Here we have a fine view of the Merced Group, — the mountain range about which the branches of the river of that name head. At Crane Flat, 6,130 feet above the sea, there is a deserted shanty and abundant feed for animals. The forests in this vicinity are superb, consisting of firs, cedars, sugar and pitch pines. There is also a small grove of the Big Trees about a mile from the Flat, in a northwesterly direction.

From here on to the Yosemite the character of the scenery begins to change, and to show indications of an approach to the higher regions of the Sierra. The larger outcrops of granite assume more or less of the dome form, and they are almost bare of vegetation. The forests become less dense, the sugar pine grows less frequent, and the firs and spruce begin to predominate over the pines. From Crane Flat to Cascade Creek is an elevated region, about 7,000 feet above the sea, and covered with snow some time after the rest of the trail has become clear. Hence a lower route has been selected, which descends Crane Creek and then skirts along the cañon of the Merced, a thousand or more feet below the one ordinarily in use later in the season. This avoiding the high ground, however, is not effected without adding a couple of miles to the distance. The two trails unite at Cascade Creek, only a short distance from the edge of the Valley. At a little distance from the trail, on the southern or right-hand side, a partial glimpse into the Yosemite may be obtained. It is not a satisfactory one, however, on account of the number of trees in the way, and the bend in the Valley itself, which cuts off the view of all the upper part. This point of view has been rather absurdly called the "Stand-Point of Silence."

Leaving our imaginary party sitting here and enjoying the cool breezes and grateful shade, we will return and conduct another set over the Mariposa trail, in order that justice may be done to "both sides."

The traveller, starting from Bear Valley for the Yosemite, passes diagonally through the whole length of the Mariposa Estate, that famous quartz-mining property which has had so many ups and downs. Before starting, however, one should take a day to ride to the summit of Mount Bullion, two miles east of Bear Valley, if he has time, and wishes for something like the distant panoramic view of the Sierra, which was described above as to be had from Pilot Peak, on the Coulterville trail. From Mount Bullion the view to the south along the crest of the Sierra is one of immense extent, the eye ranging for a hundred miles, as far as the head of the Kern and King's Rivers, along a serrated line of peaks from 12,000 to 15,000 feet in height. This view can only be had, as a rule, early in the season; for, later than May or June (according to the season), all views, from points not high up in the Sierra, begin to be obscured by the rising cloud of smoke and dust, which gradually accumulates during the summer, and finally cuts off all distant objects.

The road from Bear Valley to Mariposa passes through a region which gives as good an idea as any in the State of equal extent can of the peculiar foot-hill scenery of the Sierra Nevada. The park-like valley, with scattered oaks and pines, the latter chiefly of *Pinus Sabiniana*, the true foot-hill pine; the dark chaparral-covered hills; the ground almost hidden by a profusion of brilliant flowers and flowering shrubs in the spring, but dry, brown and dusty in the summer, still, however, invested with a certain charm by the eternal serenity of the weather; the intense heat of the sun and the refreshing coolness of the breezy shade; the nights without dew or dampness, and the days without clouds, — these are the prominent features of the lower belt of the Sierra, up to 3,000 or 4,000 feet above the sea-level.

At Mormon Bar we leave the Mariposa Estate, and, traversing a not particularly interesting, but particularly dusty, region of foot-hills, crossing numerous small branches of the Chowchilla, arrive, after twelve miles of riding, at White and Hatch's, a little over 3,000 feet above the sea-level. Here we begin to enter the real mountain region of the Sierra, to find ourselves among the tall pitch pines, and to get sniffs of cool air from the snow-banks above. From White and Hatch's to Clark's the trail ascends the Chowchilla Creek, and then crosses a high ridge forming the divide between that stream and the waters of the Merced. Nearly the whole way is among the finest forests of the Sierra, the summit on the trail being about 2,800 feet above White and Hatch's. To the left of the trail is a high granite knob, called the Devil's Mountain, not easy of ascent, but offering a fine view to the climber. From the summit the road descends rapidly, crosses Big Creek, a branch of the South Fork of the Merced, rounds the extremity of the spur which separates the creek from the river, and reaches Clark's ranch, on the banks of the South Merced, after a descent of about 1,700 feet from the summit of the trail.

At Clark's ranch we are nearly at the same elevation as the Yosemite Valley, which lies directly north at a distance of only twelve miles in a direct line.* The South Fork is here a stream 60 to 80 feet wide, clear as crystal, and heading about sixteen miles farther up, at the southeast end of the Merced Group. Mr. Clark himself is one of the pioneers of the country, and has always received travellers with that hearty hospitality and genuine kindness which makes them feel at home. The accommodations here, although not palatial, are well suited to minister to comfort. Here travellers usually remain over a day, to visit the Big Tree Grove, four miles distant, of which more in a subsequent chapter.

* Mr. Clark's house is 65 feet above the Lower Hotel in the Yosemite.

From Clark's, the trail to the Yosemite crosses the South Fork of the Merced, and ascends rapidly on to the plateau which lies between the Main Merced and the South Fork. After about six miles' travel, pretty steadily up-hill, we reach Alder Creek, 1,900 feet above Clark's, and follow this up about a mile to Empire Camp, not now inhabited, attaining here an elevation of 2,018 feet above Clark's, or about 6,000 feet above the sea-level. We are now nearly on the height of the plateau, and follow along Alder Creek to its source in a large meadow, known as Westfall's, and 3,100 feet above Clark's, or 7,100 above the sea. Here are two houses, Westfall's and Ostrander's, sometimes occupied during the summer by herders of sheep, and which have often afforded a kind of shelter, poor, but better than none, to persons overtaken by night, or too much fatigued to go farther. Usually, however, this is the lunch place, or half-way house between Clark's and the Valley, as will be easily recognized from the number of empty tin cans lying about. That we are respectably high up in the Sierra is rendered evident by the predominance of the *Pinus contorta*, a rather small tree, with its leaves short and in pairs, usually called "tamarack" by the settlers. This and the noble firs (*Picea grandis* and *amabilis*) form here almost the whole of the forests.

From Ostrander's, about half a mile northeast of Westfall's, a trail has been blazed by the Geological Survey to Sentinel Dome, of which more in the next chapter. Not far from Westfall's is a ridge, easily accessible, from which a fine view may be had of the Merced Group of mountains; Ostrander's Rocks (see map) are also an excellent point from which to survey the country.

From Westfall's to the edge of the Yosemite, the trail passes over a rolling, plateau-like country, traversing low ridges with meadows between, and rising in its highest point to 3,426 feet above Clark's, or 7,400 above the sea. At Inspiration Point the traveller gets his first view of a portion of the Yosemite, and here we will leave him, while we enter on a description of the Valley itself, leaving the account of this, and other views to be had from the outside of the walls, for another place.

The Yosemite Valley is nearly in the centre of the State north and south, and just midway between the east and west bases of the Sierra, here a little over seventy miles wide. Its shape and position will be best understood by referring to the two maps which accompany this volume. One is that prepared by Mr. Gardner for the Commissioners, and including only the Valley and its immediate surroundings; this is on a scale of two inches to a mile. The other, from the surveys of Messrs. Hoffmann and Gardner, embraces the Valley and the region adjacent for twenty miles in each direction; the scale of this is half an inch to a mile. The Valley is a nearly level area, about six miles in length and from half a mile to a mile in width, sunk almost a mile in perpendicular depth below the general level of the adjacent region. It may be roughly likened to a gigantic trough hollowed in the mountains, nearly at right angles to their regular trend; that is to say, North 60° East, the direction of the axis of the Sierra being, as before stated, North 31° West. This trough, as will be seen by reference to the map, is quite irregular, having several re-entering angles and square recesses, let back, as it were, into its sides; still, a general northeast by easterly direction is maintained in the depression, until we arrive near its upper end, when it turns sharply, at right-angles almost, and soon divides into three branches, through either of which we may, going up a series of gigantic steps, as it were, ascend to the general level of the Sierra. Down each of these branches, or cañons, descend streams, forks of the Merced, coming down the steps in a series of stupendous waterfalls. At its lower end, the Valley contracts into a narrow gorge, or cañon, with steeply inclined walls, and not having the U shape of the Yosemite, but the usual V form of California valleys.

The principal features of the Yosemite, and those by which it is distinguished from all other known valleys, are: first, the near approach to verticality of its walls; second, their great height, not only absolutely, but as compared with the width of the Valley itself; and, finally, the very small amount of *talus* or *débris* at the base of these gigantic cliffs. These are the great characteristics of the Yosemite throughout its whole length; but, besides these, there are many other striking peculiarities, and features both of sublimity and beauty, which can hardly be surpassed, if equalled, by those of any mountain valleys in the world. Either the domes or the waterfalls of the Yosemite, or any single one of them even, would be sufficient in any European country to attract travellers from far and wide in all directions. Waterfalls in the vicinity of the Yosemite, surpassing in beauty many of those best known and most visited in Europe, are actually left entirely unnoticed by travellers, because there are so many other objects of interest to be visited that it is impossible to find time for them all.

In describing the Yosemite, we will first give the necessary details in regard to the different objects of interest in and about the Valley, following it upward, and supposing the traveller to enter from the Mariposa side. In doing this, we will point out the prominent objects, in the order in which they present themselves, giving the statistics of their elevation and dimensions, so far as required or ascertained; after this has been done, we can enter into more general considerations in regard to the Valley and its surroundings, speaking of it as a whole, after due description of its parts.

In descending the Mariposa trail, a steep climb of 2,973 feet down to the bottom of the Valley, the traveller has presented to him a succession of views, all of which range over the whole extent of the principal Valley, revealing its dominant features, while at each new point of view he is brought nearer, and, as it were, more face to face with these gigantic objects. The principal points seen present themselves as follows: on the left is El Capitan, on the right the Bridal Veil Fall, coming down on the back side of the Cathedral Rocks, and in the centre the view of the Valley, and beyond into the cañon of the Tenaya Fork of the Merced: the point of the Half Dome is just visible over the ridge of which Sentinel Rock forms a part, and beyond it, in the farthest distance, Cloud's Rest is seen. A general idea of the Valley can be well obtained from this point, and in one view; but, as we ride up between the walls, new objects are constantly becoming visible, which at the lower end were entirely concealed.

Of the cliffs around the Valley, El Capitan and the Half Dome are the most striking; the latter is the higher, but it would be difficult to say which conveys to the mind the most decided impression of grandeur and massiveness. El Capitan is an immense block of granite, projecting squarely out into the Valley, and presenting an almost vertical sharp edge, 3,300 feet in elevation. (See Fig. 1.) The sides or walls of the mass are bare, smooth, and entirely destitute of vegetation. It is almost impossible for the observer to comprehend the enormous dimensions of this rock, which in clear weather can be distinctly seen from the San Joaquin plains, at a distance of fifty or sixty miles. Nothing, however, so helps to a realization of the magnitude of these masses about the Yosemite as climbing around and among them.

EL CAPITAN AND THE BRIDAL VEIL FALL.

Let the visitor begin to ascend the pile of *débris* which lies at the base of El Capitan, and he will soon find his ideas enlarged on the point in question. And yet these *débris* piles along the cliffs, and especially under El Capitan, are of insignificant size compared with the dimensions of the solid wall itself. They are hardly noticeable in taking a general view of the Valley. El Capitan imposes on us by its stupendous bulk, which seems as if hewed from the mountains on purpose to stand as the type of eternal massiveness. It is doubtful if anywhere in the world there is presented so squarely cut, so lofty, and so imposing a face of rock.

On the other side of the Valley we have the Bridal Veil Fall, unquestionably one of the most beautiful objects in the Yosemite. It is formed by the creek of the same name, which rises a few miles east of Empire

Camp, runs through the meadows at Westfall's, and is finally precipitated over the cliffs, on the west side of Cathedral Rock, into the Yosemite, in one leap of 630 feet perpendicular. The water strikes here on a sloping pile of *débris*, down which it rushes in a series of cascades for a perpendicular distance of nearly 300 feet more, the total height of the edge of the fall above the meadow at its base being 900 feet. The effect of the fall, as everywhere seen from the Valley, is as if it were 900 feet in vertical height, its base being concealed by the trees which surround it. The quantity of water in the Bridal Veil Fall varies greatly with the season. In May and June the amount is generally at the maximum, and it gradually decreases as the summer advances. The effect, however, is finest when the body of water is not too heavy, since then the swaying from side to side, and the waving under the varying pressure of the wind, as it strikes the long column of water, is more marked. As seen from a distance at such times, it seems to flutter like a white veil, producing an indescribably beautiful effect. The name "Bridal Veil" is poetical, but fairly appropriate. The stream which supplies this fall heads low down in the Sierra, far below the region of eternal snow; hence, as summer advances, the supply of water is rapidly diminished, and, by the middle or end of July, there is only a small streamlet trickling down the vertical face of the rock, over which it is precipitated in a bold curve when the quantity of water is larger. At the highest stage, the stream divides into a dozen streamlets at the base of the fall, several of which are only just fordable on horseback.

The Virgin's Tears Creek, on the other side of the Valley, and directly opposite the Bridal Veil, makes also a fine fall, over a thousand feet high, included in a deep recess of the rocks near the lower corner of El Capitan. This is a beautiful fall as long as it lasts; but the stream which produces it dries up early in the season. In quantity of water, elevation, and general effect, this fall, hardly spoken of at the Yosemite among so many grander ones, is far superior to the celebrated Staubbach of Switzerland.

Proceeding up the Valley, we find on the same side as the Bridal Veil, and a little above it, the prominent and massively sculptured pile of granite, to which the name of Cathedral Rock has been given. (See Fig. 2.) In this view the Merced River occupies the foreground; the trees in the middle ground are pitch pines from 125 to 150 feet high, and those which

Fig. 2.

CATHEDRAL ROCK.

seem to fringe the summit of Cathedral Rock like small bushes are, in reality, firs and pines, as tall as those in the Valley, or even taller. Cathedral Rock is not so high nor so massive as El Capitan, nor are its sides quite as nearly vertical. The summit is 2,660 feet above the Valley. Just beyond Cathedral Rock, on the same side, are the graceful pinnacles of rock called "The Spires." These spires are isolated columns of granite, at least 500 feet high, standing out from, but connected at the base with, the walls of the Valley. They are kept in obscurity, or brought out into wonderful relief, according to the different way the light or shadow falls upon them. The whole side of the Valley, along this part of it, is fantastically but exquisitely carved out into forms of gigantic proportions, which anywhere else, except in the Yosemite, would be considered objects of the greatest interest. From one point of view, these spires appear symmetrical, of equal height, squarely cut, and rising above the edge of the cliff behind exactly like two towers of a Gothic cathedral.

The next prominent object, in going up the Valley, is the triple group of rocks known as the Three Brothers. These rise in steps one behind the other, the highest being 3,830 feet above the Valley. From the summit of this, there is a superb view of the Valley and its surroundings. The peculiar outline of these rocks, as seen from below, resembling three frogs sitting with their heads turned in one direction, is supposed to have suggested the Indian name Pompompasus, which means, we are informed, "Leaping Frog Rocks."

Nearly opposite the Three Brothers is a point of rocks projecting into the Valley, the termination of which is a slender mass of granite, having something the shape of an obelisk, and called, from its peculiar position, or from its resemblance to a gigantic watch-tower, the "Sentinel Rock." Its form may be seen in Fig. 3, which was taken from a point on the Merced somewhat farther down the Valley. The obelisk form of the Sentinel continues down for a thousand feet or more from its summit; below that it is united with the wall of the Valley. Its entire height above the river at its base is 3,043 feet. This is one of the grandest masses of rock in the Yosemite.

From near the foot of Sentinel Rock, looking directly across the Valley, we have before us what probably most persons will admit to be, if not the most stupendous, at least the most attractive feature of the Yosemite; namely, "the Yosemite Fall" *par excellence*, that one of all the falls about the Valley which is best entitled to bear that name. The woodcut, Plate I, was taken among a group of oaks near the Lower Hotel, a point of view directly in front, and from which the various parts seem most thoroughly to be blended into one whole of surprising attractiveness. Even the finest photograph is, however, utterly inadequate to convey to the mind any satisfactory impression or realization of how many of the elements of grandeur and beauty are combined in this waterfall and its surroundings and accessories. The first and most impressive of these elements is, as in all other objects about the Yosemite, vertical height. In this it surpasses, it is believed, any waterfall

THE YOSEMITE FALL.

Fig. 3.

SENTINEL ROCK.

in the world with anything like an equal body of water. And all the accessories of this fall are of a character worthy of, and commensurate with, its height, so that everything is added, which can be, to augment the impression which the descent of so large a mass of water from such a height could not fail, by itself, to produce.

The Yosemite Fall is formed by a creek of the same name, which heads on the west side of the Mount Hoffmann Group, about ten miles northeast of the Valley. Being fed by melting snows exclusively, and running through its whole course over almost bare granite rock, its volume varies greatly at different times and seasons, according to the amount of snow remaining unmelted, the temperature of the air and the clearness or cloudiness of the weather. In the spring, when the snow first begins to melt with rapidity, the volume of water is very great; as ordinarily seen by visitors in the most favorable portion of the season, — say from May to July, — the quantity will be about that represented in the wood-cut; still later, it shrinks down to a very much smaller volume. We estimated the size of the stream at the summit of the fall, at a medium stage of water, to be twenty feet in width and two feet in average depth. Mr. J. F. Houghton measured the Yosemite Creek below the fall June 17th, 1865, and found it to be thirty-seven feet wide and twenty-five inches deep, with the velocity of about a mile an hour, giving about half a million cubic feet as passing over the fall in an hour.* At the highest stage of water there is probably three times as much as this. The vertical height of the lip of the fall above the Valley is, in round numbers, 2,600 feet, our various measurements giving from 2,537 to 2,641, the discrepancies being due to the fact that a near approach to, or a precise definition of, the place where the perpendicular portion of the fall commences is not possible. The lip or edge of the fall is a great rounded mass of granite, polished to the last degree, on which it was found to be a very hazardous matter to move. A difference of a hundred feet, in a fall of this height, would be entirely imperceptible to most eyes.

The fall is not in one perpendicular sheet. There is first a vertical descent of 1,500 feet, when the water strikes on what seems to be a projecting ledge; but which, in reality, is a shelf or recess, almost a third of a mile back from the front of the lower portion of the cliff. From here the water finds its way, in a series of cascades, down a descent equal to 626 feet perpendicular, and then gives one final plunge of about 400 feet on to a low *talus* of rocks at the base of the precipice. The whole arrangement and succession of the different parts of the fall can be easily understood by ascending to the base of the Upper Fall, which is a very interesting and not a difficult climb, or from Sentinel Dome, on the opposite side of the Valley, where the spectator is at a considerable distance above its edge.† As the various

---

* Our measurements gave about 220 cubic feet as the amount of water passing over the fall in one second.

† The exact distance from the Sentinel Dome across in a straight line to the edge of the Upper Yosemite Fall is two and a half miles.

portions of the fall are nearly in one vertical plane, the effect of the whole is nearly as grand, and perhaps even more picturesque, than it would be if the descent were made in one leap from the top of the cliff to the level of the Valley. Nor is the grandeur or beauty of the fall perceptibly diminished, by even a very considerable diminution of the quantity of water from its highest stage. One of the most striking features of the Yosemite Fall is the vibration of the upper portion from one side to the other, under the varying pressure of the wind, which acts with immense force on so long a column. The descending mass of water is too great to allow of its being entirely broken up into spray; but it widens out very much towards the bottom, — probably to as much as 300 feet, at high water, the space through which it moves being fully three times as wide. This vibratory motion of the Yosemite and Bridal Veil falls is something peculiar, and not observed in any others, so far as we know; the effect of it is indescribably grand, especially under the magical illumination of the full moon.

The cliff a little east of the Yosemite Fall rises in a bold peak to the height of 3,030 feet above the Valley; it can be reached up Indian Cañon, a little farther east, and from this point a magnificent view of the whole region can be obtained. The ascent to the summit of the fall and the return to the Valley can be made in one day, but only by good mountain climbers.

Following up the Valley for about two miles above the Yosemite Falls, we find that the main portion of it comes to an end, and that it suddenly branches out in three distinct but much narrower *cañons*, as they would be called by Californians, each of which, however, has some new wonders to disclose. The Merced River keeps the middle one of these, and its course is here about the same that it was below, or nearly west; it holds this direction nearly up to the base of the Mount Lyell Group, where it heads, between the main crest of the Sierra and the parallel subordinate or side range called by us the Merced or Obelisk Group. In the left hand, or northwesterly cañon, the Tenaya Fork of the Merced comes down, and in the right hand, or southwesterly one, the South Fork,* or the Illilouette.

---

* This is the "South Fork of the Middle Fork," and not the main South Fork, which flows by Clark's Ranch. To avoid confusion, it will be well to call it by the Indian name, Illilouette, one not yet much in use in the Valley.

At the angle where the Yosemite branches we have, on the north side, the rounded columnar mass of rock called the Washington Column, and immediately to the left of it the immense arched cavity called the "Royal Arches," and over these is seen the dome-shaped mass called the North Dome, shown in Fig. 4.

Fig. 4.

THE NORTH DOME.

The North Dome, rising to 3,568 feet above the Valley, is one of those rounded masses of granite which are not uncommon in the Sierra Nevada. These dome-shaped masses are somewhat characteristic of all granitic regions, but are nowhere developed on so grand a scale as in the Sierra. An examination of the figure will show that the North Dome is made up of huge concentric plates of rock, overlapping each other, in such a way as to absolutely prevent an ascent on the side presented to the Valley; to the north, however, the Dome runs out in a long ridge, as represented on

Top of Half Dome.   Cathedral Peak.   Vernal Fall   Mount Broderick

THE CAÑON OF THE MERCED AND THE VERNAL FALL.

the map, and from that side there is not the slightest difficulty in getting to the summit.

The concentric structure of the North Dome is well seen in the Royal Arches, which are, in fact, a sort of appendage to its base. This peculiarity of structure pervades the whole mass of rock, and it is evident that these arches have been formed by the slipping down of immense plates of granite, the size of the cavity thus left being enormous, but not easily measured. The arches and the column, at the angle of the main Valley and the Tenaya Cañon, seem as if intended to form a base of adequate magnitude and grandeur for the support of the Dome which rests upon them.

The Half Dome, on the opposite side of the Tenaya Cañon, is the loftiest and most imposing mass of those considered as part of the Yosemite. It is not so high as Cloud's Rest, but the latter seems rather to belong to the Sierra than to the Yosemite. The Half Dome is in sight, in the distance, as we descend the Mariposa trail, but is not visible in the lower part of the Valley itself; it is seen first when we come to the meadow opposite Hutchings's. The form of the Half Dome may be understood from Fig. 5 and Plate II. In the one it is seen flatwise or in front, from below; and in the other nearly edgewise, from above. It is a crest of granite, rising to the height of 4,737 feet above the Valley, perfectly inaccessible, being probably the only one of all the prominent points about the Yosemite which never has been, and never will be, trodden by human foot. The summit of the Half Dome runs in a northeast and southwest direction, parallel with the cañon; it rises on the southwest side with a grand, regular dome-like form, but falls off rapidly in a series of steps as it descends to the northeast. At right angles with this, or crosswise of the mass, the section is very peculiar. On the side fronting Tenaya Cañon, it is *absolutely vertical* for 2,000 feet or more from the summit, and then falls off with a very steep slope, of probably 60 or 70 degrees, to the bottom of the cañon. This slope, however, is not, as one would suppose, a *talus* of fragments fallen from above; it is a mass of granite rock, part and parcel of the solid structure of the Dome; the real *débris* pile at the bottom is absolutely insignificant in dimensions compared with the Dome itself. On the opposite face the Half Dome is not absolutely vertical; it has a rounded form at the top, and grows more and more steep at the bottom. In Plate II. we see only the top

Fig. 5.

THE HALF DOME.

of the Half Dome and a portion of the back, the view being taken from a point not exactly in a line with its edge. The whole appearance of the mass is that of an originally dome-shaped elevation, with an exceedingly steep curve, of which the western half has been split off and become engulfed. This geological theory of its formation appears to have forced itself upon those who gave it the name "Half Dome," which is one that seems to suggest itself, at the first sight of this truly marvellous crest of rock. From the upper part of the Valley, and from all the heights about it, the Half Dome presents itself as an object of the most imposing grandeur. It has not the massiveness of El Capitan, but is more astonishing, and probably there are few visitors to the Valley who would not concede to it the first place among all the wonders of the region. Even the most casual observer must recognize in it a new revelation of mountain grandeur. Those who have not seen it could never comprehend its extraordinary form and proportions, not even with the aid of photographs. It is entirely unique in the Sierra Nevada; and, so far as we know, in the world. The only possible rival would be the Matterhorn. Each is unique in its way; but the forms of the two are so different that they will hardly bear comparison.

Farther up the cañon of the Tenaya is a beautiful little lake called "Mirror Lake," an expansion of the Tenaya Fork. It is frequently visited, and best early in the morning, for the purpose of getting the reflection from its unruffled surface of a noble overhanging mass of rock, to which the name of Mount Watkins has been given, as a compliment to the photographer who has done so much to attract attention to this region.

Still farther up the Tenaya Fork, on the right-hand side, is "Cloud's Rest," the somewhat fanciful designation of a long, bare, steep, and extremely elevated granite ridge, which connects the Valley with the High Sierra. This point is one of the few which have not been measured by the Geological Survey; it is perhaps a thousand feet higher than the Half Dome, or nearly 10,000 feet above the sea-level.

Following up the Tenaya Fork cañon, we find the creek coming down in a series of cascades and waterfalls through an almost impassable gorge; but through which access may be had, by good climbers, to the trail from Big Oak Flat to Mono Lake. It is, however, not passable for animals.

We return now to the cañon of the main Merced River, which also has its own peculiar wonders to disclose. Leaving the Yosemite Valley proper, at the angle spoken of before, where the three cañons unite, we follow up the Merced, soon crossing the Illilouette, which carries perhaps a third or a quarter as much water as the main river. Rising rapidly on a trail which runs along near the river, over the *talus* of great angular masses fallen from above, we ride a little less than a mile, and nearly to the base of the first of the two great falls made by the Merced in coming down from the level of the plateau above into the Yosemite Valley. In doing this, the river descends, in two miles, over 2,000 feet, making, besides innumerable cascades, two grand falls, which are among the greater attractions of the Yosemite, not only on account of their height and the large body of water in the river during most of the season, but also on account of the stupendous scenery in the midst of which they are placed.

The first fall reached in ascending the cañon is the Vernal, a perpendicular sheet of water with a descent varying greatly with the season. Our measurements give all the way from 315 to 475 feet for the vertical height of the fall, between the months of June and October. The reason of these discrepancies seems to lie in the fact that the rock near the bottom is steeply inclined, so that a precise definition of the place where the perpendicular part ceases is very difficult amid the blinding spray and foam. As the body of water increases, the force of the fall is greater, and of course it is thrown farthest forward when the mass of water is greatest. Probably it is near the truth to call the height of the fall, at the average stage of water in June or July, 400 feet. The rock behind this fall is a perfectly square cut mass of granite extending across the cañon, and it is wonderful to see, at low water, how little the eroding effect of the river has had to do with the formation of the cañon and fall. It would seem as if causes now in action had little or nothing to do with the formation of this step in the descent of the Merced to any Valley below. In Plate II. we see the Vernal Fall in the distance, a little to the right of the centre of the picture; beyond it, and still a little farther to the right, is Mount Broderick or the "Cap of Liberty."

The path up the side of the cañon near the fall winds around and along a steeply sloping mountain-side, always wet with the spray, and consequently rather slippery in places. Ladies, however, find no great difficulty in passing, with the aid of friendly arms, and protected by stout boots and india-rubber clothing brought from the hotel. The perpendicular part of the ascent is surmounted by the aid of ladders, which should be replaced by a substantial and well-protected staircase. At the summit of the fall the view down the cañon, as well as in the opposite direction, is extremely fine. A remarkable parapet of granite runs along the edge of the Vernal Fall for some distance, just breast-high, and looking as if made on purpose to afford the visitor a secure position from which to enjoy the scene.

From the Vernal Fall up stream, for the distance of about a mile, the river may be followed, and it presents a succession of cascades and rapids of great beauty. As we approach the Nevada Fall, the last great one of the Merced, we have at every step something new and impressive. The view represented in the annexed woodcut (Fig. 6) was taken a little above the

THE CAP OF LIBERTY AND THE NEVADA FALL.

a grand mass of rock, isolated and nearly perpendicular on all sides, rising perhaps 2,000 feet above its base, and little inferior to the Half Dome in grandeur. It has been climbed, and has on its summit, according to Mr. Hutchings's statement, a juniper-tree of enormous diameter.

The Nevada Fall is, in every respect, one of the grandest waterfalls in the world, whether we consider its vertical height, the purity and volume of the river which forms it, or the stupendous scenery by which it is environed. The fall is not quite perpendicular, as there is near the summit a ledge of rock which receives a portion of the water and throws it off with a peculiar twist, adding considerably to the general picturesque effect (see woodcut).

A determination of the height of the fall was not easy, on account of the blinding spray at the bottom, and the uncertainty of the exact spot where the water strikes. Indeed, this seems to vary in the Nevada as well, although not so much, as in the Vernal Fall. Our measurements made the Nevada from 591 to 639 feet, at different times and seasons. To call the Vernal 400 and the Nevada 600 feet, in round numbers, will be near enough to the truth. The descent of the river in the rapids between the two falls is nearly 300 feet.

In the cañon of the South Fork, or Illilouette, there is a fine fall estimated at 600 feet high. It is seen from a point on the trail from the Hotel to Mirror Lake, although but rarely visited by travellers, the cañon being rough and difficult to climb. A trail should be made up this gorge, to give access to the fall, and to the superb views to be had of the back of the Half Dome, the Vernal Fall, and other interesting points.

Having thus run rapidly through the list of objects in the Valley best known and most likely to be visited, we will give a more systematic and general account of the Yosemite, — its botany, topography, and geology ; this will enable us to bring forward some interesting considerations which could not so well be introduced in a detailed enumeration, in a geographical order, of the points of interest.

The Yosemite Valley, proper — that is to say, what would be considered by the visitor as naturally included under that designation — may be described as consisting of three parts, the bottom of the Valley, or the actual Valley, the *talus* or *débris* slope, and the walls, or the vertical or nearly vertical solid rock. Each of these parts will be noticed in order. First, the bottom, or Valley proper. This is a nearly level area, having a gentle slope, with the river, to the southwest, of only 35 feet between the junctions of the Tenaya Fork and the Bridal Veil Creek with the main river, four miles and a half in a straight line. The width of the space between the *débris* slopes is very variable. In the upper half of the Valley it averages somewhat less than half a mile. A little below the Three Brothers it closes to an eighth of a mile in width ; and between El Capitan and Cathedral Rock the river "cañons," to use a California phrase, meaning that the Valley is narrowed down, so that there is only just room for the river to pass. Below this, it opens out again, and forms two charming little patches of meadow, of about 20 acres each in extent. There are, altogether, 1,141 acres of land in the Valley proper, of which 745 are meadow, and the remainder a sandy soil, a little more elevated, partly covered with a sparse growth of forest trees and partly with pertinacious ferns. The elevation of the bottom of the Valley above the sea-level is, in round numbers, 4,000 feet. The mean of our observations, in June, was 4,046 feet; those taken by Miss Sproat, in October, gave, as calculated by Colonel R. S. Williamson, 3,935 feet. The mean of these results is 3,990 feet, and that is probably not far from the truth. Through the Valley flows the Merced River, about 70 feet in width, making many sharp and curiously angular bends, touching the *talus* first on one side and then on the other.

Along the banks of the river, and over the adjacent rather swampy meadows, we find a somewhat varied vegetation, according to the locality, the narrow portions of the Valley differing considerably from the broader ones. In the former, near the falls, there is a dense growth of alder (*Alnus viridis*), which sometimes forms quite a large tree, with ash-colored bark; associated with this are small trees of *Rhamnus Menziesii*, remarkable for its large and sombre leaves. A few willows, the Douglas spruce (*Abies Douglasii*), and, in the upper part of the Valley, an occasional sugar pine, are also found in this position. Where the Valley widens out, and the river banks become lower, so that sloughs and swamps are formed, the Balm of Gilead poplar (*Populus balsamifera*) comes in; this is a common tree in the Valley, and is usually mistaken for the cottonwood; with this occur large willows and abundance of the Douglas spruce, and also the *Azalea occidentalis*, whose superb white and fragrant flowers form one of the charms of the Valley. *Hellenium grandiflorum*, Nutt., with its numerous yellow flowers, is a showy and conspicuous plant on and near the river banks. The meadows are swampy, with a deep peaty soil; their vegetation consists chiefly of carices or sedges and a few coarse grasses (*Calamagrostis Canadensis*, Beauv., *Phragmites communis*, L., *Glyceria nervata*, Trin.). In a small pond on Mr. Hutchings's farm, the yellow pond-lily (*Nuphar advena*, Ait.) occurs. At the upper part of the side cañons and near the falls, the Vernal especially, the cryptogamic vegetation is most abundantly developed. Where the rocks are kept moistened by the spray, numerous mosses thrive; and even on the hill-slopes, as far as the moisture reaches, the peat moss (*Sphagnum*) grows.

The shelving rocks in such positions are decorated with several species of most graceful ferns. About the Vernal Fall, the following species occur, all of rare beauty: *Adiantum pedatum*, Kaulf., *Pellœa densa*, Hook., *P. Bridgesii*, Hook., *P. mucronata*, Eat., *Cheilanthes gracillima*, Eat., *Polypodum Californicum*, Kaulf., *Aspidium argutum*, Kaulf., and *Cystopteris fragilis*, Bernh.

The sandy region of the Valley proper forms a connecting strip along the edge of the rocky *talus*, on both sides of the river. It is quite irregular in width; but it makes up the largest portion of the Valley above Indian Cañon. It has evidently been formed by the disintegration and washing down of the finer portions of the *débris* from the walls. The soil is a coarse, loose, deep sand, containing but little vegetable matter, and becoming finer, more compact, and more fertile as it approaches the river. This is peculiarly the arboriferous belt of the Valley, and various portions of its area exhibit different characters of vegetation to correspond with the differences of soil. On the drier and looser portions, the pitch (or yellow) pine (*P. ponderosa*) and the bastard cedar (*Libocedrus decurrens*) are the most abundant and characteristic trees; both these species occur of considerable size and of fine proportions, the pines being usually from 125 to 150 feet high. Below the Bridal Veil Fall, near the *débris*, the fir (*Picea grandis*), a noble tree, comes in; near the swampy land, the black oak (*Q. Sonomensis*) is abundant. The sandy region also bears a great number and variety of shrubs and undergrowth: among these are: the *Cornus Nuttallii*, with its showy white flowers, three inches in diameter; *Rubus Nutkanus*, the most beautiful of the raspberries, and found from Lake Superior west; also the characteristic California shrub, manzanita (*Arctostaphylos glauca*). Among the lower shrubs are: the wild rose (*Rosa blanda*); *Pentstemon lætus*, with its beautiful blue flowers; *Hosackia grandiflora*, also with brilliant flowers; also, in places, the *Frangula Californica*, forming dense thickets; the same is true of the low willow. The common brake (*Pteris aquilina*) is very abundant and sometimes very large. The curious *Spraguea umbellata*, one of the most characteristic flowers of the Valley, is also abundant in the sandy region. In places, especially below the Bridal Veil Fall, *Comandra umbellata*, *Silene compacta*, and *Chænactis achillæfolia* cover the ground. An examination of the different woodcuts will show how the vegetation is distributed in the Valley, and the most characteristic trees will easily be recognized.

The meadows and sandy portions, described above as constituting the bottom of the Valley, contain all the land in the Yosemite which can be utilized for any purpose, such as building or cultivation. The *talus* or *débris*, the second great division, forms steeply sloping masses of rocky fragments piled along the base of the cliffs, on both sides and from one end of the Valley to the other. Only in a very few places do the nearly vertical walls come squarely down to the level of the Valley, without any intervening *talus*. These places are easily recognized upon the map. The *talus*, however, is everywhere of insignificant height compared with the cliffs themselves, this being, as before remarked, one of the characteristic features of the Valley. The *débris* lies chiefly in the receding or re-entering angles, and in the cañons or gorges down which the smaller streams flow into the Valley. It is least conspicuous around some of the more prominent and elevated projecting points, as the Three Brothers, El Capitan, and the Cathedral Rock. Singularly enough, there is also very little *débris* at the foot of the Yosemite Fall; while, on the opposite side of the Valley, the *talus* is exceptionally wide. On examining the woodcuts, it will be noticed at once how little the *talus* has to do with producing the general effect of the Yosemite; in most of them it can hardly be recognized as existing at all.

The most characteristic tree of the *débris* piles is, perhaps, the mountain live-oak (*Q. chrysolepis*, Liebm.), which is associated, in the higher portions, with the common shrubby evergreen oak of the higher Sierras, perhaps the *Q. vaccinifolia* of Kellogg. In the vicinity of the points where small streams come over the precipices, we find the Oregon maple (*Acer macrophyllum*, Pursh), with its large and deeply cut leaves, and, in the higher portions of the *débris*, another maple (*Acer glabrum*, Torr.), a shrub, 10 or 15 feet high, whose delicate branches, long peduncled leaves, and clusters of reddish seed make it an object conspicuous for its beauty. Near the base of the *débris*, where the streams of the smaller waterfalls emerge, the California laurel (*Tetranthera Californica*) occurs as a small tree, with smooth brilliant evergreen foliage and aromatic odor. Among the smaller plants, we have several beautiful species of *Pentstemon*; one with brilliant scarlet flowers (*P. Menziesii*, Hook.) is very conspicuous. *Bahia confertiflora*, a low shrub, with densely clustered yellow flowers, is also abundant. A number of species of grasses, of great interest to the botanist, also occur in this position; and in the crevices of the rocks the beautiful little fern *Cheilanthus gracillima*, with several others equally graceful, occurs.

The slope along the descent by which the Mariposa trail winds into the Valley offers, also, an interesting and peculiar grouping of species. Oaks, pines, and firs make up the forest, and with these is a profusion of flowering shrubs, some of which are very showy. Among these are the *Ceanothus integerrimus*, H. & A., with its dense clusters of white or pale-blue and fragrant flowers, often called the "beauty of the Sierra"; the *C. divaricatus*, Nutt., with fragrant blue flowers; *Philadelphus Californicus*, with large white flowers; an occasional "poison oak" (*Rhus diversiloba*, T. & G.); also the "snow plant" or "ice plant" (*Sarcodes sanguinea*, Torr.), the whole of which is of a brilliant red, like a tongue of flame issuing from the ground; and, especially, the great white Lily of the Sierra (*Lilium Umpquaensis?*), perhaps the most superb and deliciously fragrant flower of California.

The salient and most striking points in the walls of the Yosemite have already been passed rapidly in review. The whole Valley, however, is surrounded by this wall, and the objects particularly noticed were only such portions of it as attract general and immediate attention, owing to some peculiarity of form or position. Every portion of the Yosemite wall is sublime; and where there is so much to be seen, and where every object can be seen from so many different points of view, there is hardly any limit to the combinations of the different elements of landscape beauty, which can be obtained by change of position and change of illumination. The color of the granite of the walls is a light gray, — brilliantly white, generally, when the sun's light is reflected from it. It is, in places, diversified with veins of a brighter or deeper hue; but these patches of color are not conspicuous enough to produce much effect. More character is given by the vertical parallel lines of darker color, — gray, brown, and black, — with which portions of the walls are striped. These are the result of the flowing down of water, in the line of most direct descent, over the face of the cliffs, carrying organic matter in solution or suspension. These stains are very conspicuous, and not at all ungraceful, on the Royal Arches, as well as on El Capitan and other vertical cliffs. The general effect of the cliffs, as to color, is dazzling in the sunlight; but it is the brilliancy of cold colors, not of warm ones, and the various oil paintings of the Yosemite, representing a rich golden haze as pervading and giving its hue to everything in the Valley, are simply and entirely untrue to nature. The beauty of color comes rather from the intensity of the contrast of the gray rock with the brilliant vegetation of the Valley bottom, and, in a less degree, with that of the cañons and the edge of the cliffs.

Although there is no exit from the Yosemite for a mounted traveller, except by one of the two trails winding up the steep slope at the lower end of the Valley, there are several places where a footman can find his way out without any difficulty, except that naturally resulting from a climb up a steep slope of angular rocks, equal in vertical rise to 3,000 feet and more. Tourists have occasionally climbed up Indian Cañon to the head of the Yosemite Fall (see map), and also up the gorge by the side of Sentinel Rock, to get to its summit and to the Sentinel Dome. There are places where one could climb up, apparently, near the Cathedral, a little below El Capitan, and between El Capitan and the Three Brothers; but we are not aware that they have ever been tried. Persons who are not accustomed to climbing, and especially ladies, are strongly advised to ride out of the Valley on the regular trails, when they wish to make excursions on the outside, rather than risk getting over-fatigued in performing acrobatic feats, which are not at all necessary to enable one to see and enjoy the whole region. More than one person, however, has climbed, stocking-footed in some particularly ticklish places, up the cliff on the left-hand side of the Yosemite Fall, along the ledges, when there is room, if not for a foothold, at least for a toe-hold. We have never heard that any serious accident has happened to visitors to the Yosemite, but too much caution cannot be used, by ladies especially, in regard to over-fatiguing themselves.

Some general statements as to the waterfalls of the Yosemite, in addition to what has already been said on this subject, may here be introduced. The principal falls about the Valley have already been described; but there are several others not yet mentioned which are worthy of notice. It is only early in the season, while the snow on the summits immediately adjacent to the Valley is melting, that the "grandes eaux" of this national park can be said to be in play. Indeed, at such times, and especially after the first few warm days in the spring, there are large numbers of small streams discharging themselves over the cliffs, and each, of course, producing a waterfall proportionate in picturesque effect to the amount of water it furnishes. Of these minor falls, there are several which continue for a considerable time; others are quite short-lived. The Virgin's Tears Fall is one of the finest of the former; in 1867 it was quite a fine sight in June. There is another, nearly opposite, on a stream called Meadow Brook, which is well seen by those coming into the Valley on the Mariposa trail early in the season. A stream heading at Ostrander's Rocks comes down near Sentinel Rock, in a kind of " Buttermilk Fall," or series of step-like cascades, until all the snow at its head has disappeared. The fall over the Royal Arches also keeps itself alive for some time, with quite a body of water coming down from the North Dome, and on the opposite side the Sentinel Dome also furnishes its quota towards keeping up the high display of the Yosemite. There are as many reasons, then, as there are waterfalls in the Valley, why the traveller should visit the Yosemite early in the season. It is true that some visitors who have arrived too late to see the falls in their grandeur have voted them, if not "humbugs," at least non-essential to the glory of the Yosemite. They have been so much impressed with the mighty cliffs and domes that they have not conceived it possible that such sublimity could be heightened by the introduction of any additional features. It is true that the Valley has about it, aside from its waterfalls, that which will amply repay the traveller for the time and labor required for his visit; but it is not true that such natural objects as the Yosemite, the Vernal, or Nevada Falls, seen with all their glorious surroundings, do not immeasurably enhance the attractions of the Valley. The traveller should endeavor, if possible, to visit the region just as the last snow is disappearing from the plateau; and, as soon as the trail is made on a lower level, as suggested above, he will be able to do so with ease and comfort at a considerably earlier period than now. May, June, and July are the most favorable months; and even April, in some years, would not be too early. Of the principal falls in the Valley, only the Vernal and Nevada continue in existence through the season. The Yosemite and the Bridal Veil shrink almost to nothing by August or September. This is the result of the peculiar climate of California, by which rains are, even in the mountains, almost entirely dispensed with during the six summer months, so that the streams have to be fed exclusively from melting snow. As every rule has its exception, it sometimes happens here that heavy thunder-showers around the Valley raise the streams suddenly, in midsummer, to the highest point of their winter flow. This occurred in 1867, when a violent thunder-storm at the head of the Merced, in June, raised the South Fork at Clark's ranch and the Yosemite Creek several feet, within half an hour. This rain-fall was limited to a quite small area; but a very large amount of water must have fallen in a short space of time. It was probably of the nature of one of those violent deluges, which not unfrequently occur in California, and which are generally known as "cloud-bursts."

Some comparison of the principal falls in the Yosemite with the most celebrated ones in other parts of the world will be of interest to the tourist, as enabling him to form an opinion as to their relative attractiveness. There are several circumstances to be taken into consideration, however, in a comparison of waterfalls. Absolute height and quantity of water are undoubtedly the two important elements; but all the accessories have a share in producing the general effect. The fall is the picture; but the value of it is wonderfully heightened or diminished, according to the more or less picturesque character of the frame in which it is set. Exactly what the relative importance of height and volume is, in producing the effect in different waterfalls, it is not easy to say. There are those on whom Niagara, with its immense mass of water, would produce a greater effect than the Yosemite, with its ten times greater height and its much more than ten times diminished volume. Others, again, would consider the higher fall as much the more attractive, in spite of its comparatively small body of water. Niagara and the Zambesi are typical falls for volume; but probably no one has seen both of these, so as to be able to institute a valuable comparison between them.

The falls visited by tourists, in Europe, are very numerous; but they all belong to the type of those which impress by their height and not by their volume, resembling in this respect the Yosemite Fall. The most celebrated are those of Norway and Switzerland; but the highest of all is that of Gavarnie, in the Pyrenees, in which the vertical descent is 1,266 feet. In this fall the quantity of water is only just enough to form a dozen thin streams, trickling down the face of the rock, with one, a little larger than the others, which swings off as a white cord, twice broken by projecting ledges, and entirely dissipated in spray before it reaches the bottom. It is plain enough, then, that the fall of Gavarnie will not compare with that of the Yosemite either in volume or height. The fall of the Staubbach, in Switzerland, is about the height of the Bridal Veil; but the quantity of water is extremely small, so that the effect is insignificant, compared even with that of the Virgin's Tears. The fall of the Aar, at Handek, makes a fine show, but is not, by any means, as imposing as the Vernal Fall, being inferior to it in elevation and in volume, and of course much behind the Nevada in both respects.

The Vöring Foss, in Norway, is generally admitted to be the finest waterfall in Europe; its volume is about that of the Aar at Handek, and its height is estimated at 850 feet. It has never been measured, for it falls into an inaccessible chasm, which is only just as wide as the stream itself. As it can only be viewed from above, much of the impressiveness of the fall is lost. Mr. Brace, the author of the "Norse-Folk," who is probably the only person who has seen both the Yosemite Valley and the Vöring Foss, considers the Norwegian falls to be far inferior to those of California.

Asia and South America seem poorly provided with waterfalls; at least, there are few described which can be mentioned in comparison with those of Europe and North America; and it is likely that, if any of surpassing grandeur existed in those countries, they would have become known before this time. We are disposed to believe that a majority of cultivated lovers of natural scenery would admit the Yosemite Fall to surpass any in the world, as presenting the most perfect combinations of all the elements of the picturesque. Certainly, taking the whole region of the Yosemite together, with its five great falls, the lowest 400 feet and the highest 2,600, it must be allowed that, in this particular kind of scenery, it is a locality without a rival in the world.

Although the Valley is, at present, almost inaccessible in the winter, and, indeed, entirely so to those who are not up in travelling on snow-shoes, it is not unlikely that the time will soon come when a visit to it at that season will be considered as the "regular thing" for tourists, and when proper facilities for getting there will be provided. The views, at the time when the snow is still lying deep on the surrounding plateau, and thundering down in frequent avalanches from the domes and over the walls of the Valley; or, a little later, when the streams are filled to repletion and pour themselves over the cliffs in literally unnumbered cascades; when the Merced becomes a mad torrent, and hurries down its 2,000 feet of vertical descent in one wild mass of spray-enveloped waters, — all this is, as described by those who have seen it, of surpassing grandeur. The accumulation of ice at the base of the upper part of the Yosemite Fall is also spoken of as a most impressive feature in the winter view. The frozen spray forms a vast conical mass, rising sometimes to the height of a hundred feet or more, from which the falling water, rebounding, is shot off in graceful curves, forming an immense bouquet, each drop of which sparkles like a diamond in the sun.

All will recognize in the Yosemite a peculiar and unique type of scenery. Cliffs absolutely vertical, like the upper portions of the Half Dome and El Capitan, and of such immense height as these, are, so far as we know, to be seen nowhere else. The dome form of mountains is exhibited on a grand scale in other parts of the Sierra Nevada; but there is no Half Dome, even among the stupendous precipices at the head of the King's River. No one can avoid asking, What is the origin of this peculiar type of scenery? How has this unique valley been formed, and what are the geological causes which have produced its wonderful cliffs, and all the other features which combine to make this locality so remarkable? These questions we will endeavor to answer, as well as our ability to pry into what went on in the deep-seated regions of the earth, in former geological ages, will permit.

Most of the great cañons and valleys of the Sierra Nevada have resulted from aqueous denudation, and in no part of the world has this kind of work been done on a larger scale. The long-continued action of tremendous torrents of water, rushing with impetuous velocity down the slopes of the mountains, has excavated those immense gorges by which the chain of the Sierra Nevada is furrowed, on its western slope, to the depth of thousands of feet. This erosion, great as it is, has been done within a comparatively recent period, geologically speaking, as is conclusively demonstrated in numerous localities. At the Abbey's Ferry crossing of the Stanislaus, for instance, a portion of the mass of Table Mountain is seen on each side of the river, in such a position as to demonstrate that the current of the lava which forms the summit of this mountain once flowed continuously across what is now a cañon over 2,000 feet deep, showing that the erosion of that immense

Fig. 7.

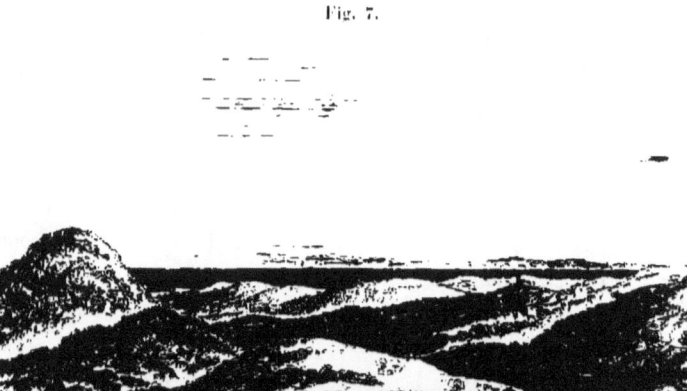

DISTANT VIEW OF TABLE MOUNTAIN.

gorge has all been effected since the lava flowed down from the higher portion of the Sierra. This event took place, as we know from the fossil bones and plants embedded under the volcanic mass, at a very recent geological period, or in the latter part of the Tertiary epoch. Some even claim that it happened since the appearance of man on the earth; but this, although not impossible, remains yet to be proved. Figures 7 and 8 and Plate III. show the varying forms and picturesque character of some of these outliers of volcanic materials. Fig. 7 represents Table Mountain in Tuolumne County, as seen from a point distant about twelve miles in a southeasterly direction. The long straight line of its upper edge, destitute of vegetation and dark colored, will easily be recognized. Fig. 8 represents a picturesque outlier of volcanic materials near Railroad Flat in Calaveras County, which is quite surrounded by ridges of this character, rising 600 to 800 feet above the general level of the region, and indicating clearly the great erosion which has taken place since a recent geological period.

The eroded cañons of the Sierra, however, whose formation is due to the action of water, never have vertical walls, nor do their sides present the peculiar angular forms which are seen in the Yosemite, as, for instance, in El

VOLCANIC RIDGES NEAR SILVER MOUNTAIN.

FORT HILL, — NEAR RAILROAD FLAT.

Capitan, where two perpendicular surfaces of smooth granite, more than 3,000 feet high, meet each other at a right angle. It is sufficient to look for a moment at the vertical faces of El Capitan and the Bridal Veil Rock, turned down the Valley, or away from the direction in which the eroding forces must have acted, to be able to say that aqueous erosion could not have been the agent employed to do any such work. The squarely cut re-entering angles, like those below El Capitan, and between Cathedral Rock and the Sentinel, or in the Illilouette cañon, were never produced by ordinary erosion. Much less could any such cause be called in to account for the peculiar formation of the Half Dome, the vertical portion of which is all above the ordinary level of the walls of the Valley, rising 2,000 feet, in sublime isolation, above any point which could have been reached by denuding agencies, even supposing the current of water to have filled the whole Valley.

Much less can it be supposed that the peculiar form of the Yosemite is due to the erosive action of ice. A more absurd theory was never advanced than that by which it was sought to ascribe to glaciers the sawing out of these vertical walls and the rounding of the domes. Nothing more unlike the real work of ice, as exhibited in the Alps, could be found.

Besides, there is no reason to suppose, or at least no proof, that glaciers have ever occupied the Valley or any portion of it, as will be explained in the next chapter, so that this theory, based on entire ignorance of the whole subject, may be dropped without wasting any more time upon it.

The theory of erosion not being admissible to account for the formation of the Yosemite Valley, we have to fall back on some one of those movements of the earth's crust to which the primal forms of mountain valleys are due. The forces which have acted to produce valleys are complex in their nature, and it is not easy to classify the forms which have resulted from them in a satisfactory manner. The two principal types of valleys, however, are those produced by rents or fissures in the crust, and those resulting from flexures or foldings of the strata. The former are usually transverse to the mountain chain in which they occur; the latter are more frequently parallel to them, and parallel to the general strike of the strata of which the mountains are made up. Valleys which have originated in cross fractures are usually very narrow defiles, enclosed within steep walls of rocks, the steepness of the walls increasing with the hardness of the rock. It would be difficult to point to a good example of this kind of valley in California; the famous defile of the Via Mala in Switzerland is one of the best which could be cited. Valleys formed by foldings of the strata are very common in many mountain chains, especially in those typical ones, the Jura and the Appalachians. Many of the valleys of the Coast Ranges are of this order. A valley formed in either one of the ways suggested above may be modified afterwards by forces pertaining to either of the others; thus a valley originating in a transverse fissure may afterwards become much modified by an erosive agency, or a longitudinal flexure valley may have one of its sides raised up or let down by a "fault" or line of fissure running through or across it.

If we examine the Yosemite to see if traces of an origin in either of the above ways can be detected there, we obtain a negative answer. The Valley is too wide to have been formed by a fissure; it is about as wide as it is deep, and, if it had been originally a simple crack, the walls must have been moved bodily away from each other, carrying the whole chain of the Sierra with them, to one side or the other, or both, for the distance of half a mile. Besides, when a cliff has been thus formed, there will be no difficulty in recognizing the fact, from the correspondence of the outlines of the two sides; just as, when we break a stone in two, the pieces must necessarily admit of being fitted together again. No correspondence of the two sides of the Yosemite can be detected, nor will the most ingenious contriving, or lateral moving, suffice to bring them into anything like adaptation to each other. A square recess on one side is met on the other, not by a corresponding projection, but by a plain wall or even another cavity. These facts are sufficient to make the adoption of the theory of a rent or fissure impossible. There is much the same difficulty in conceiving of the formation of the Valley by any flexure or folding process. The forms and outlines of the masses of rock limiting it are too angular, and have too little development in any one direction; they are cut off squarely at the upper end, where the ascent to the general level of the country is by gigantic steps, and not by a gradual rise. The direction of the Valley, too, is transverse to the general line of elevation of the mountains, and not parallel with it, as it should be, roughly at least, were it the result of folding or upheaval.

In short, we are led irresistibly to the adoption of a theory of the origin of the Yosemite in a way which has hardly yet been recognized as one of those in which valleys may be formed, probably for the reason that there are so few cases in which such an event can be absolutely proved to have occurred. We conceive that, during the process of upheaval of the Sierra, or, possibly, at some time after that had taken place, there was at the Yosemite a subsidence of a limited area, marked by lines of "fault," or fissures crossing each other somewhat nearly at right angles. In other and more simple language, the bottom of the Valley sank down to an unknown depth, owing to its support being withdrawn from underneath, during some of those convulsive movements which must have attended the upheaval of so extensive and elevated a chain, no matter how slow we may imagine the process to have been. Subsidence, over extensive areas, of portions of the earth's crust, is not at all a new idea in geology, and there is nothing in this peculiar application of it which need excite surprise. It is the great amount of vertical displacement for the small area implicated which makes this a peculiar case; but it would not be easy to give any good reason why such an exceptional result should not be brought about, amid the complicated play of forces which the elevation of a great mountain chain must set in motion.

By the adoption of the subsidence theory for the formation of the Yosemite, we are able to get over one difficulty which appears insurmountable with any other. This is, the very small amount of *débris* at the base of the cliffs, and even, at a few points, its entire absence, as previously noticed in our description of the Valley. We see that fragments of rock are loosened by rain, frost, gravity, and other natural causes, along the walls, and probably not a winter elapses that some great mass of detritus does not come thundering down from above, adding, as it is easy to see from actual inspection of those slides which have occurred within the past few years, no inconsiderable amount to the *talus*. Several of these great rock-avalanches have taken place since the Valley was inhabited. One which fell near Cathedral Rock is said to have shaken the Valley like an earthquake. This abrasion of the edges of the Valley has unquestionably been going on during a vast period of time; what has become of the detrital material? Some masses of granite now lying in the Valley — one in particular near the base of the Yosemite Fall — are as large as houses. Such masses as these could never have been removed from the Valley by currents of water; in fact, there is no evidence of any considerable amount of aqueous erosion, for the cañon of the Merced below the Yosemite is nearly free from detritus, all the way down to the plain. The falling masses have not been carried out by a glacier, for there are below the Valley no remains of the moraines which such an operation could not fail to have formed.

It appears to us that there is no way of disposing of the vast mass of detritus, which must have fallen from the walls of the Yosemite since the formation of the Valley, except by assuming that it has gone down to fill the abyss, which was opened by the subsidence which our theory supposes to have taken place. What the depth of the chasm may have been we have no data for computing; but that it must have been very great is proved by the fact that it has been able to receive the accumulations of so long a period of time. The cavity was, undoubtedly, occupied by water, forming a lake of unsurpassed beauty and grandeur, until quite a recent epoch. The gradual desiccation of the whole country, the disappearance of the glaciers and the filling up of the abyss to nearly a level with the present outlet, where the Valley passes into a cañon of the usual form, have converted the lake into a valley with a river meandering through it. The process of filling up still continues, and the *talus* will accumulate perceptibly fast, although a long time must elapse before the general appearance of the Valley will be much altered by this cause, so stupendous is the vertical height of its walls, and so slow their crumbling away, at least as compared with the historic duration of time.

Lake Tahoe and the valley which it partly occupies we conceive also to be, like the Yosemite, the result of local subsidence. It has evidently not been produced by erosion; its depth below the mountains on each side, amounting to as much as 3,000 feet, forbids this idea, as do also its limited area and its parallelism with the axis of the chain. The Lake is still very deep, over 1,000 feet; but how deep it was originally, and how much detritus has been carried into it, we have no data for even crudely estimating.

CHAPTER IV.

THE HIGH SIERRA.

HAVING, in the last chapter, given as full a description of the Yosemite Valley as our space will permit, we proceed next to call the reader's attention to the higher region of the Sierra Nevada — the Alps of California, as the upper portion of this great chain of mountains is sometimes called; this region we designate, for convenience, as the "High Sierra." It is, however, especially the elevated valleys and mountains which lie above and near the Yosemite that we wish to describe, and to endeavor to bring to the reader's notice, as this is not only a region central and easy of access, but one extremely picturesque, and offering to the lover of high mountain scenery every possible inducement for a visit. By adding a few more days to the time required for a trip to the Yosemite, the tourist may make himself acquainted with a type of scenery quite different from that of countries usually visited by pleasure travellers, and may enjoy the sight of as lofty snow-covered peaks, and as grand panoramic views of mountain and valley, as he can find in Switzerland itself. This region of the High Sierra in California is hardly yet opened to visitors, so far as the providing for them of public accommodations is concerned, for there is not a hotel, nor a permanently inhabited house, anywhere near the crest of the Sierra, between the Silver Mountain road on the north and Walker's Pass on the south; but such is the mildness of the summer, and so steady is the clearness of the atmosphere in the Californian high mountains, that, with a very limited amount of preparation, one may make the tour outside of the Yosemite almost without any discomforts, and certainly without any danger. In the Sierra Nevada, the entire absence of severe storms during the summer, and the almost uninterrupted serenity of the sky, particularly invite to pleasure travel. The worrying delays and the serious risks of Alpine travel, caused by long-continued rains and storms of wind and hail, with their attendant avalanches of snow and rocks, are unknown in the Californian high mountains, and we have camped by the week together, in the constant enjoyment of the finest weather, at elevations which would seem too great for anything but hardship and discomfort.

A comparison of the Swiss and Californian Alpine scenery is not easy, and yet it seems natural to wish to give some idea of the most striking features of the Sierra by referring for comparison, or contrast, to the mountain scenery of Switzerland, which has become the very focus of pleasure travel for the civilized world.*

The much smaller quantity of snow and ice in the Sierra, as compared with regions of equal elevation in Switzerland, is the most striking feature of difference between the mountains of the two countries. In the Sierra we see almost exactly what would be presented to view in the Alps, if the larger portion of the ice and snow-fields were melted away. The marks of the old glaciers are there; but the glaciers themselves are gone. The polished surfaces of the rocks, the moraines or long trains of detritus, and the striae engraved on the walls of the cañons, — these speak eloquently of such an icy covering once existing here as now clothes the summits of the Alps.

Another feature of the Sierra, as compared with the Alps, is the absence of the "Alpen," or those grassy slopes which occur above the line of forest vegetation, between that and the eternal snow, and which have given their names to the mountains themselves. In the place of these, we have in the California mountains the forests extending quite up to the snow-line in many places, and everywhere much higher than in the Alps. The forests of the Sierra, and especially at elevations of 5,000 to 7,000 feet, are magnificent, both in the size and beauty of the trees, and far beyond any in the Alps; they constitute one of the most attractive features of the scenery, and yet they are somewhat monotonous in their uniformity of type, and they give a sombre tone to the landscape, as seen from a distance in their dark shades of green. The grassy valleys, along the streams, are extremely beautiful, but occupy only a small area; and, especially, they do not produce a marked effect in the distant views, since they are mostly concealed behind the ranges, to one looking over the country from a high point.

* There are probably ten times as many persons in California who have travelled for pleasure in Switzerland, as among these most interesting portions of the Sierra.

The predominating features, then, of the High Sierra are sublimity and grandeur, rather than beauty and variety. The scenery will perhaps produce as much impression, at first, as that of the Alps, but will not invite so frequent visits, nor so long a delay among its hidden recesses. Its type is different from that of the Swiss mountains, and should be studied by those who wish to see Nature in all her variety of mountain gloom and mountain glory. The many in this country who do not have the opportunity of seeing the Alps should not miss the Sierra, if it be in their power to visit it.

For a journey around the Yosemite, or in any portion of the High Sierra, mules or horses may be hired at Bear Valley, Mariposa, or Coulterville; and the services of some one who will act as guide can be obtained, usually, at either of these places. But there are, as yet, no regular guides for the high mountains, and travel must increase considerably before any such will be found. A good pedestrian will often prefer to walk, and will pack his baggage on a horse or mule. For convenience and enjoyment, the party should consist of several persons. A good supply of blankets and of provisions, with a few simple cooking utensils, an axe, a light tent, substantial woollen clothes, and, above all, or rather under all, a pair of boots " made on honor," with the soles filled with nails, — these are the principal requisites. The guide will initiate the unpractised traveller into the mysterious art of "packing" a mule or horse, an accomplishment which can only be acquired by actual practice, but one on the skilful performance of which much of the traveller's comfort depends. Those who are familiar with woods-life in California, or elsewhere, can easily find their way about with the help of the maps contained in this volume.

It will be the principal object of this chapter to describe the region of the High Sierra adjacent to the Yosemite, and this will first be done; after which, we will add a brief description of some other less known portions of the Sierra, in the hope that travellers may be induced to visit them, and, perhaps, to give to the world some of their experience, for the benefit of future tourists. And, for convenience, we will first describe the trip which is most likely to be made by those visiting the Yosemite; namely, an excursion around the Valley, on the outside, one which will reveal much that is of great interest, occupying but few days, and which can be made mostly on beaten trails, without the slightest difficulty or danger. We cannot but believe that the time will soon come when hundreds, if not thousands, will every year visit this region, and that it will become as well known as the valleys and peaks of the Bernese Oberland.

In making the circuit of the Yosemite, as here proposed, the traveller is supposed to start from the Valley itself, leaving it on the north side, and following the Mono trail to Soda Springs, camping there and ascending Mount Dana, then returning by the trail from Mono to Mariposa, passing behind Cloud's Rest and the Half Dome, through the Little Yosemite, across the Illilouette, by the Sentinel Dome, then to Westfall's and back into the Valley, or to Clark's Ranch, as may be desired, the whole trip occupying about a week.

Leaving the Valley, the traveller ascends to the plateau by the Coulterville trail; but, instead of keeping on the trail back to that place, turns sharp to the right just after passing the Boundary corner, taking the trail formerly considerably used by mule-trains between Big Oak Flat and Aurora. This trail was of some importance at the time that the Esmeralda District was in favor with mining speculators; for, although it rises to the elevation of over 10,700 feet above the sea-level, yet, there being an abundance of feed at the various flats and meadows on the route, — which, as they were not claimed or fenced in, were free to all, — it offered a more eligible route for large trains of mules than the passes farther north, where all the grass was taken possession of by settlers, and where, consequently, feed must be purchased. In 1863 all the meadows on the Silver Mountain road (the one next north of the Sonora Pass road) were claimed; there were several public houses on the route, and a public conveyance over it; but, at that time, there was not a house or a settler on the Mono trail anywhere between Deer Flat, twenty-two miles below the Yosemite, and the eastern base of the Sierra, near Mono Lake; nor is there now, so far as we are informed. The traveller, therefore, will not be able to telegraph, in advance of his arrival, for rooms at the sumptuous hotel at the next station; but he will find grassy meadows in which to pasture his animals, scattered along the route at convenient intervals, will have an abundance of ice-cold water, and, drawing on his saddle-bags for his own rations, with unlimited command of free fuel, he will find both novelty and delight in his entire independence of hotel bills, and in knowing that he is not in danger of being crowded out of his "accommodations."

The first good camping-ground, after leaving the Valley on the Mono trail, is in the neighborhood of the Virgin's Tears Creek, and from here the highest of the Three Brothers may be easily reached, in an hour or two. There is no trail blazed as yet; but the shortest and best way can easily be found, in the absence of a guide, by the aid of the map. From this commanding point, almost 4,000 feet above the Valley, the view is extremely fine, the Merced River and green meadows which border it seeming to be directly under the observer's feet. Probably there is no better place from which to get a bird's-eye view of the Yosemite Valley itself; and, in respect to the distant view of the Sierra to be had from the summit of the Three Brothers, it can only be said, that, like all the others which can be obtained from commanding positions around the Valley, it seems, while one is enjoying it, to be the finest possible. At the time of our visit to this region in 1866, we climbed a commanding ridge just north of our camp on the Virgin's Tears Creek, from which a noble panoramic view of the Sierra was had. It was just at sunset, and the effect of color which was produced by some peculiar condition of the atmosphere, and which continued for at least a quarter of an hour, was something entirely unique and indescribably beautiful. The whole landscape, even the foreground and middle ground, as well as the distant ranges, became of a bright Venetian-red color, producing an effect which a painter would vainly attempt to imitate by any color or combination of colors. It was unlike the "Alpine glow," so often seen in high mountains; for, instead of being confined to the distant and lofty ranges, it tinged even the nearest objects, and not with shades of rose-color and purple, but with a uniform tint of brilliant, clear red.

After crossing the Virgin's Tears, the next creek is that which forms the Yosemite Falls, and which is about two miles farther on. The trail crosses this creek a little above a small meadow, where one can camp, and from which the brink of the fall and the summit of the cliff overhanging it on the east may be visited. A couple of miles farther on is a high meadow called Deer Park, on which there was some snow even in the latter part of June, 1863; for we are here nearly 8,500 feet above the sea-level. Descending a little, we soon reach Porcupine Flat, a small meadow of carices, 8,173 feet above tide water, and a good camping-ground for those who wish to visit Mount Hoffmann.

Mount Hoffmann is the culminating point of a group of elevations, very conspicuous from various points about the Yosemite, and especially from the Mariposa trail and from Sentinel Dome, looking directly across the Valley and to the north of it. It is about four miles northwest of Porcupine Flat, and can be reached and ascended without the slightest difficulty. The ridge to which it belongs forms the divide between the head-waters of Tenaya and Yosemite Creeks, the latter heading in several small lakes which lie immediately under the bold mural face of the range, which is turned to the northwest. The summit is 10,872 feet above the sea-level, and is a bare granitic mass, with a gently curving slope on the south side, but falling off in a grand precipice to the north.

The view from the summit of Mount Hoffmann is remarkably fine, and those who have not time, or inclination, to visit the higher peaks of the main ridge of the Sierra are strongly advised to ascend this, as the trip from the Yosemite and back need only occupy two or three days; and no one who has not climbed some high point above the Valley can consider himself as having made more than a distant acquaintance with the High Sierra. This is a particularly good point for getting an idea of the almost inaccessible region of volcanic masses lying between the Tuolumne River and the Sonora Pass road, of which a characteristic instance is given in Fig. 9, which represents some of the great tables resting on the granite and 3,000 feet above the adjacent valley, the dark mass of lava in the centre of the picture being fully 700 feet thick. The number of distinct peaks, ridges, and tables, visible in that direction, crowded together, is too great to be counted. The grand mass of Castle Peak is a prominent and most remarkably picturesque object. This mountain was thus named by Mr. G. H. Goddard, about ten years ago, at which time he ascended, by estimate, to within 1,000 feet of the summit, and calculated it to be 13,000 feet in elevation above the sea-level.* Messrs. King and Gardner made several attempts to climb it, but did not succeed in getting to the top, although Mr. Goddard thinks it can easily be reached from the north. By some unaccountable mistake, the name of Castle Peak was afterwards transferred to a rounded and not at all

---

* Mr. Goddard's measurement was made with an aneroid barometer, and subsequent examinations along his route, by the Geological Survey, indicate that his figures are about 500 feet too great. Castle Peak is probably between 12,000 and 12,500 feet high.

Fig. 9.

VOLCANIC TABLES ON GRANITE.

castellated mass about seven miles north of Mount Dana; but we have returned the name to the peak to which it belongs, and given that of General Warren, the well-known topographer and engineer, to the one on which the entirely unsuitable name of Castle Peak had become fixed.

From Porcupine Flat and Mount Hoffmann, we look directly south on to the fine group of mountains lying southeast of the Yosemite and called by us the Obelisk Group, which will be fully described further on in this chapter. (See Plate IV.) It is a conspicuous feature in the scenery of the region about the Yosemite.

Lake Tenaya, the head of the branch of the Merced of the same name, is the next point of interest on the trail, and is about six miles east-northeast of Porcupine Flat. It is a beautiful sheet of water, a mile long and half a mile wide. The trail passes around its east side, and good camping-ground can be found at the upper end in a fine grove of firs and pines. The rocks in the vicinity all exhibit in the most remarkable degree the concentric structure peculiar to the granite of this region. At the head of the Lake is a very conspicuous conical knob of smooth granite, about 800 feet

THE OBELISK GROUP — FROM PORCUPINE FLAT.

high, entirely bare of vegetation, and beautifully scored and polished by former glaciers. The traces of the existence of an immense flow of ice down the valley now occupied by Lake Tenaya begin here to be very conspicuous. The ridges on each side of the trail are worn and polished by glacial action nearly to their summits, so that travelling really becomes difficult for the animals on the pass from the valley of the Tenaya into that of the Tuo-

Fig. 10.

CATHEDRAL PEAK, FROM NEAR LAKE TENAYA.

lumne, so highly polished and slippery are the broad areas of granite over which they have to pick their way. A branch of the great Tuolumne glacier flowed over into the Tenaya Valley through this pass, showing that the thickness of the mass of ice was much more than 500 feet, which is the difference of level between the summit of the pass and the Tuolumne River. As the glacial markings are seen on the rocks around Lake Tenaya at an elevation of fully 500 feet above its level, it is certain that the whole thickness of the ice in the Tuolumne Valley must have been at least 1,000 feet. The summit of the pass is 9,070 feet above the sea-level.

The trail descends into the valley of the Tuolumne, winding down under the brow of the Cathedral Peak group, a superb mass of rock, which first becomes conspicuously visible to the traveller just before reaching Lake

Tenaya. (See Fig. 10.) This is one of the grandest landmarks in the whole region, and has been most appropriately named. As seen from the west and southwest, it presents the appearance of a lofty mass of rock, cut squarely down on all sides for more than a thousand feet, and having at its southern end a beautiful cluster of slender pinnacles, which rise several hundred feet above the main body. It requires no effort of the imagination to see the

Fig. 11.

CATHEDRAL PEAK, FROM TUOLUMNE VALLEY.

resemblance of the whole to a Gothic cathedral; but the majesty of its form and its vast dimensions are such, that any work of human hands would sink into insignificance beside it. Its summit is at least 2,500 feet above the surrounding plateau, and about 11,000 feet above the sea-level. From the Tuolumne River Valley, on the east, the Cathedral Peak presents a most attractive appearance; but has quite lost the peculiar resemblance which was so conspicuous on the other side. (See Fig. 11 and Plate V.)

Unicorn Peak.   Cathedral Peak.

UPPER TUOLUMNE VALLEY — FROM SODA SPRINGS, LOOKING SOUTH.

The valley of the Tuolumne, into which the Mono trail now descends (see map), is one of the most picturesque and delightful in the High Sierra. Situated at an elevation of between 8,000 and 9,000 feet above the sea-level, surrounded by noble ranges and fantastically shaped peaks which rise from 3,000 to 4,000 feet higher, and from which the snow never entirely disappears, traversed by a clear rapid river, along which meadows of carices and clumps of pines and firs alternate, the effect of the whole is indeed most superb. The main portion of the valley is about four miles long, and from half to a third of a mile wide. At its upper end it forks, the Mono trail taking the left-hand branch, or that which comes down from Mount Dana, while the right-hand fork, or that which enters from the southeast, is the one heading on the north side of Mount Lyell (see map), about eight miles above the junction of the two branches. Soda Springs, on the north side of the Tuolumne, near the place where the Mono trail descends into the valley, offers an agreeable camping-ground, and many other pleasant spots can be found between this and the head of the pass. The springs furnish a mild chalybeate water, slightly impregnated with carbonic acid gas, and rather pleasant to the taste. They are elevated thirty or forty feet above the river, and are 8,680 feet above the sea. From this point the view in all directions is a magnificent one. The Cathedral Peak Group is one of the most conspicuous features in the landscape, the graceful, slender form of the dominating peak being always attractive, from whichever side it is seen. What resembled the spires of a cathedral, in the distant view from the west, near Lake Tenaya, is now seen to be two bare pyramidal peaks, rising precipitously from the forest-clothed sides of the ridge to the height of about 2,300 feet above the valley. (See Plate V.) Farther east the range is continued in a line of jagged peaks and pinnacles, too steep for the snow to remain upon them, and rising above great slopes of bare granite, over which, through the whole summer, large patches of snow are distributed, in sheltered places and on the north side. One of these peaks has a very peculiar horn-shaped outline, and hence was called Unicorn Peak. This range trends off to the southeast and unites with the grand mass of the Mount Lyell Group, which forms the dominating portion of the Sierra in this region.

The vicinity of Soda Springs, and, indeed, the whole region about the head of the upper Tuolumne, is one of the finest in the State for studying the traces of the ancient glacier system of the Sierra Nevada. The valleys of both the Mount Lyell and the Mount Dana forks exhibit abundant evidence of having been filled, at no very remote period, with an immense body of moving ice, which has everywhere rounded and polished the surface of the rocks, up to at least a thousand feet above the level of the river. This polish extends over a vast area, and is so perfect that the surface

Fig. 12.

GLACIER-POLISHED ROCKS, UPPER TUOLUMNE VALLEY.

is often seen from a distance to glitter with the light reflected from it, as from a mirror. Not only have we these evidences of the former existence of glaciers, but all the phenomena of the moraines — lateral, medial, and terminal — are here displayed on the grandest scale.

To the northeast of Soda Springs, a plateau stretches along the southwestern side of the crest of the Sierra, with a gentle inclination towards the river, rising gradually up to a rugged mass of peaks, of which Mount Conness is the highest. The plateau lies at an elevation of between 9,000 and 10,000 feet; it has clumps of *Pinus contorta* scattered over it, and is furrowed by water-courses, which are not very large. The whole surface of this is most beautifully polished and grooved, except where covered with the piles of *débris*, which stretch across it in long parallel lines, and which are the medial moraines of the several side glaciers, which formerly united with the main one, coming down from the gorges and cañons of the great mass of the Sierra above. About a mile below the springs are the remains of a terminal moraine, stretching across the valley; it is not very conspicuous, except from the fact that it bears a scattered growth of pines, contrasting beautifully with the grassy and level area above and below. A mile and a half lower down, a belt of granite, a mile or more wide, extends across the valley; over this the river falls in a series of cascades, having a perpendicular descent of above a hundred feet in all. This granite belt is worn into many knobs, some of which are a hundred feet high and over; between these are great grooves and channels worn by ice, and their whole surface, to the very summit, is scratched and polished, the markings being parallel with the present course of the river.

Below this is another grassy field, and then the river enters a cañon, which is about twenty miles long, and probably inaccessible through its entire length; at least we have never heard of its being explored, and it certainly cannot be entered from its head. Mr. King followed this cañon down as far as he could, to where the river precipitated itself down in a grand fall, over a mass of rock so rounded on the edge, that it was impossible to approach near enough to look over into the chasm below, the walls on each side being too steep to be climbed. Where the cañon opens out again, twenty miles below, so as to be accessible, a remarkable counterpart of the Yosemite Valley is found, called the Hetch-Hetchy Valley, which will be described farther on. Between this and Soda Springs there is a descent in the river of 4,500 feet, and what grand waterfalls and stupendous scenery there may be here it is not easy to say. Although we have not succeeded in getting into this cañon, it does not follow that it cannot be done. Adventurous climbers, desirous of signalizing themselves by new discoveries, should try to penetrate into this unknown gorge, which may perhaps admit of being entered through some of the side cañons coming in from the north, and which must exhibit stupendous scenery. The region north of this cañon, as far as the Sonora road across the Sierra, is wonderfully wild and difficult of access. Our parties made some attempt to penetrate it, and to reach Castle Peak, but without success, partly owing to the great difficulty of finding feed for the animals.

Just before reaching the head of the great cañon, there is an isolated granite knob in the valley, rising to the height of about 800 feet above the river, and beautifully glacier-polished to its very summit. At this point the great glacier of the Tuolumne must have been at least a mile and a half wide and over 1,000 feet thick. From this knob the view of the valley and the surrounding mountains is one hardly surpassed in interest and grandeur. Plate VI. reproduces a sketch taken from this point looking towards the Cathedral Peak Group, and shows the fine mass of elevations to the southwest. In the lower part of the valley are the smooth and glittering surfaces of granite, indicating the former existence of the glacier; above this, on either hand, the steep slopes of the mountains, clad with a sombre growth of pines (*Pinus contorta*), and beyond, still higher up, the great snow-fields, above which rises the Unicorn Peak, and many other nameless ones, in grand contrast with the dome-shaped masses seen, in the farthest distance, in the direction of Lake Tenaya.

Of all the excursions which can be made from Soda Springs, the one most to be recommended is the ascent of Mount Dana, as being entirely without difficulty or danger, and as offering one of the grandest panoramic views which can be had in the Sierra Nevada; those who wish to try a more difficult feat can climb Mount Lyell or Mount Conness.* Since the visit of the Geological Survey to this region, in 1863, several parties have ascended Mount Dana, riding nearly to the summit on horseback, and there can be no doubt that the ascent will, in time, become well known, and popular among tourists. As it is rather too hard a day's work to go from

---

* Mount Dana was named after Professor J. D. Dana, the eminent American geologist; Mount Lyell, from Sir Charles Lyell, whose admirable geological works have been well known to students of this branch of science, in this country, for the past thirty years. Mount Conness bears the name of a distinguished citizen of California, now a United States Senator, who deserves, more than any other person, the credit of carrying the bill organizing the Geological Survey of California, through the Legislature, and who is chiefly to be credited for another great scientific work, the Survey of the 40th Parallel.

CATHEDRAL PEAK GROUP — UPPER TUOLUMNE VALLEY.

Soda Springs to the summit of Mount Dana and back in a day, it will be convenient to move camp to the base of the mountain, near the head of the Mono Pass. The distance from the springs to the summit of the pass is about ten miles in a straight line, and perhaps twelve in following the trail. A convenient place for camping, and from which to ascend Mount Dana, is at a point about three miles from the summit of the pass, on the left bank of the stream and near the junction of a small branch, coming in from the slopes of Mount Dana to unite with the main river, which heads in the pass itself and along the ridges to the southeast of it. This camp is 9,805 feet above the sea, and about a thousand feet below the summit of the pass, which is 10,765 feet in elevation.

An examination of the map will give a better idea than any verbal explanation can do of the character and position of the subordinate members of the crest of the Sierra in this region. A jagged line of granite pinnacles runs from the head of the San Joaquin River northwest, for about twenty miles, beginning at the Minarets and ending at Cathedral Peak. Mount Ritter, Mount Lyell, and Mount Maclure are the only points in this range that we have named;* they are all about 13,000 feet high.

From Mount Lyell starts off a grand spur connecting with the Obelisk Group Range, which runs parallel with the Mount Lyell Range and about ten miles from it. About the same distance from the latter, in the opposite direction from the Obelisk Group, is another serrated line of peaks, of which Mount Conness is the culminating point. Connecting the Mount Lyell and the Mount Conness ranges, and forming the main divide of the Sierra, in this part, is a series of elevations which have rounded summits and rather gently sloping sides, contrasting in the most marked manner with the pinnacles and obelisks of the other ranges. This portion of the Sierra runs north and south, and has as its dominating mass Mount Dana, which appears to be the highest point anywhere in this region, and which was, for a considerable time, supposed by us to be the highest of the whole Sierra, with the exception of Mount Shasta. Mount Dana and Mount Lyell are so nearly of the same height that the difference falls within the limits of possible

---

* Ritter is the name of the great German geographer, the founder of the science of modern comparative geography. To the pioneer of American geology, William Maclure, one of the dominating peaks of the Sierra Nevada is very properly dedicated.

instrumental error; but on levelling, with a pocket-level, from one to the other, the former seemed to be a little the higher of the two.

Mount Dana is the second peak north of the pass; the one between that mountain and the pass is called Mount Gibbs. Between the two is a gap somewhat lower than the Mono Pass, but descending too steeply on the eastern side to admit of use without considerable excavation. There is also another pass on the north side of Mount Dana, as represented on the map; this is about 600 feet lower than the Mono Pass, and might probably be made available with a small expenditure. From the summit everywhere to the east, the descent is exceedingly rapid; that through "Bloody Cañon," as the east slope of the Mono Pass is called, lets the traveller down 4,000 feet in three miles. The total descent from the summit of Mount Dana to Mono Lake is 6,773 feet, and the horizontal distance only six miles, or over 1,100 feet fall to the mile.

We ascended Mount Dana twice from the south side without difficulty, sliding down on the snow for a considerable portion of the way, on the return, making a descent of about 1,200 feet in a couple of minutes. We have been told, however, that the approach to the summit from the opposite side is much easier, and that it is even possible to ride a horse nearly to the top from the northwest. The height was determined by us to be 13,227 feet, and it need hardly be added that the view from the summit is sublime. Every tourist who wishes to make himself acquainted with the high mountain scenery of California should climb Mount Dana; those who ascend no higher than the Yosemite, and never penetrate into the heart of the mountains, should never undertake to talk of having seen the Sierra Nevada; — as well claim an intimate acquaintance with the Bernese Oberland after having spent a day or two in Berne, or with Mont Blanc after visiting Geneva. The Yosemite is something by itself; it is not the High Sierra, it belongs to an entirely different type of scenery. From Mount Dana, the innumerable peaks and ranges of the Sierra itself, stretching off to the north and south, form, of course, the great feature of the view. To the east, Mono Lake lies spread out, as on a map, at a depth of nearly 7,000 feet below, while beyond it rise, chain above chain, the lofty and, here and there, snow-clad ranges of the Great Basin, — a region which may well be called a wilderness of mountains, barren and desolate in the highest degree, but possessing many of the

Mount Dana. Glacier-polished surfaces.
CREST OF THE SIERRA, LOOKING EAST FROM ABOVE SODA SPRINGS.

elements of the sublime, especially vast extent and wonderful variety and grouping of mountain forms.

The upper part of Mount Dana is not granite, as are almost all the surrounding peaks. It is made up of slate, very metamorphic near the summit, and showing, farther down, especially on the south side, alternating bands of bright green and deep reddish-brown, and producing a very pleasing effect, by the contrast of these brilliant colors, especially when the surface is wet. This belt of metamorphic rock is seen to extend for a great distance to the north, giving a rounded outline to the summits in that direction, of which Mount Warren, about six miles distant and 13,000 feet high, as near as we could estimate, is one of the most prominent. The contrast between the contours of the metamorphic summits of the Sierra and the granitic ones will be seen on comparing Plates VII. and VIII.

Along the western and southern slopes of Mount Dana the traces of ancient glaciers are very distinct, up to a height of 12,000 feet. In the gap directly south of the summit a mass of ice must once have existed, having a thickness of at least 800 feet, at as high an elevation as 10,500 feet. From all the gaps and valleys of the west side of the range, tributary glaciers came down, and all united in one grand mass lower in the valley, where the medial moraines which accumulated between them are perfectly distinguishable, and in places as regularly formed as any to be seen in the Alps at the present day. On the eastern side of the pass, also, the traces of former glacial action are very marked, from the summit down to the foot of the cañon; and there are several small lakes which are of the kind known as "moraine lakes," formed by the damming up of the gorge by the terminal moraines left by the glacier as it melted away and retreated up the cañon.

Of the high peaks adjacent to Mount Dana, Mount Warren was ascended by Mr. Wackenreuder, and Mount Conness by Messrs. King and Gardner. The latter was reached by following a moraine which forms, as Mr. King remarks, a good graded road all the way round from Soda Springs to the very foot of the mountain. The ascent was difficult and somewhat hazardous, the approach to the summit being over a knife-blade ridge, which might be trying to the nerves of the uninitiated in mountain climbing. The summit is 12,692 feet above the sea-level, and is of granite, forming great concentric plates dipping to the west. Of course, the view, like all from the dominant peaks of this region, is extensive, and grand beyond all description.

Our party also ascended the Mount Lyell fork, following up the valley of that stream. From near the head of it, the sketch was taken which is reproduced in Plate VIII. and which gives a good idea of the Alpine character of this portion of the Sierra. The highest point of the group was

Fig. 13.

SUMMIT OF MOUNT LYELL.

ascended by Messrs. Brewer and Hoffmann; but they were unable to reach the very summit, which was found to be a sharp and inaccessible pinnacle of granite rising above a field of snow. (See Fig. 13.) By observations taken at a station estimated to be 150 feet below the top of this pinnacle, Mount Lyell was found to be 13,217 feet high. The ascent was difficult, on account of the body of snow which had to be traversed, and which was softened by the sun, so that climbing in it was very laborious. This trouble might have been obviated, however, by camping nearer the summit and ascending before the sun had been up long enough to soften the snow. The culminating peaks of Mount Lyell have a gradual slope to the northeast; but to the south and southwest they break off in precipices a thousand feet or more in height. Between these cliffs, on that side, a vast amphitheatre is included, once the birthplace of a grand glacier, which flowed down into the cañon of the Merced. From this point, the views of the continuation of the chain to the southeast are magnificent. Hundreds of points, in that direction, rise to an elevation of over 12,000 feet, mostly in jagged pinnacles of granite, towering above extensive snow-fields, with small plateaus between them. This continuation of the range to the southeast of Mount Lyell was afterwards visited by another party, and the peak called on the map Mount Ritter was ascended, as will be noticed farther on, after completing the tour around the Yosemite.

If the traveller has ascended Mount Dana, he will probably desire to return down the Tuolumne Valley and continue his journey on the trail leading south of Cloud's Rest, to the Little Yosemite and Sentinel Dome, and so back to Clark's Ranch. This trail strikes directly south from the crossing of the Tuolumne, a little below Soda Springs, and passes close under Cathedral Peak, on the west side, then along the back, or east side of Cloud's Rest, and down into the Little Yosemite Valley, as it is called.

This is a flat valley or mountain meadow, about four miles long and from half a mile to a mile wide. It is enclosed between walls from 2,000 to 3,000 feet high, with numerous projecting buttresses and angles, topped with dome-shaped masses. At the upper end of the valley it contracts to a V-shaped gorge, through which the Merced rushes with rapid descent, over huge masses of *débris*. The Little Yosemite Valley is a little over 6,000 feet above the sea-level, or 2,000 above the Yosemite, of which it is a kind of continuation, being on the same stream, — namely, the main Merced, — and only a short distance above the Nevada Fall, from the summit of which easy access may be had to it, whenever the bridge across the river between the Vernal and Nevada Falls has been rebuilt. This bridge, which was carried away in the winter of 1867 – 68, obviated the necessity of a very circuitous and difficult climb, to get from the base of the Nevada Fall to its summit, the ascent being quite easy on the north side of the river. On the south side, about midway up the Valley, a cascade comes sliding down in a clear sheet over a rounded mass of granite; it was estimated at 1,200 feet in height. The concentric structure of the granite is beautifully marked in the Little Yosemite; the curious rounded mass, called the Sugar Loaf, is a good instance of this.

The trail, leaving the Little Yosemite, crosses the divide between the Merced and the Illilouette, then the last-named stream, passing to the west of Mount Starr King, another of those remarkable conical knobs of granite, of which there is quite a group in this vicinity. From various points in the upper part of the Yosemite Valley, from which one can look up the Illilouette Cañon, the summit of Mount Starr King is just visible in the distance, nearly concealed behind another of these domes or cones, the two being with difficulty to be distinguished from each other, except when the sunlight happens to fall on one and not on the other, which is necessarily something of rather rare occurrence. Starr King is the steepest cone in the region, with the exception of the Half Dome, and is exceedingly smooth, having hardly a break in it; the summit is quite inaccessible, and we have not been able to measure its height.

There is nothing more of particular interest in this vicinity, nor before reaching Westfall's meadows, except the Sentinel Dome. This may be visited from Ostrander's, from which a trail has been blazed, or from the Illilouette Valley direct, on the return route. Horses may be ridden nearly to its summit, which is a great rounded mass of granite, with a few straggling pines on it. The view it commands is indeed sublime. Looking directly across the Yosemite, we have on the left the snow-covered mass of Mount Hoffmann, and, nearly under it, the rounded summit of the North Dome, and another similar mass of granite near it. In the centre of the field, the view extends directly up the Tenaya Cañon, past the stupendous vertical face of the Half Dome, on to the bare regular slope of Cloud's Rest, while on the opposite side of the cañon we see Mount Watkins, and, in the distance, the serrated crest of the Sierra. The points next to the left of Cloud's Rest, and directly over the Tenaya Cañon, belong to the Cathedral Peak and Unicorn Peak ranges, which are such prominent features in the view from Soda Springs. The tip of Cathedral Peak is just seen rising above the intervening ranges. Beyond, in the farthest distance, we have the higher range of Mount Conness and the adjacent peaks. The Half Dome is the great feature in this view, and no one can form any conception of its grandeur who has only seen it from the Valley below. On the Sentinel Dome we are 4,150 feet above the Valley; but still lack 587 feet of being as high as the summit of the Half Dome.

Facing the east, we have directly in front the Nevada Fall, with the Cap of Liberty on the left of it. Just above the latter we look into the Little Yosemite, and see a spot of its level floor, surrounded by bare, shelving granite masses. On the extreme left is a small portion of the bare side of the Half Dome, and the farthest point to the right is the Obelisk, or Mount Clark, the most western and dominating point of the Merced Group, its sides streaked with snow. In the extreme distance is the mass of mountains which we have called the Mount Lyell Group.*

Looking towards the southeast, we have a grand view of the whole of the Merced Group, in the distance, the Obelisk on the left, and the three other principal peaks to the right. Just midway between the Sentinel Dome and the Obelisk is the curious elevation called Mount Starr King, mentioned before as being an extremely steep, bare, inaccessible cone of granite, surrounded by several others of the same pattern, but of smaller dimensions.

The Sentinel Dome may easily be reached by the traveller to the Yosemite, by stopping over a day, on the way to or from the Valley, at Westfall's meadow. It makes just a pleasant day's excursion to ride to the Dome and back, with a few hours to remain on the summit. But if one is in a hurry, it is possible to make the trip and return in time to reach either Clark's or the Yosemite before night. To visit this region and not ascend Sentinel Dome, is a mistake; only those who have had the pleasure of making this excursion can appreciate how much is lost by not going there.

There is one point overhanging the Valley, about half a mile northeast of the Sentinel Dome, and directly in a line with the edge of the Half Dome. This is called Glacier Point, and the view from it combines perhaps more elements of beauty and grandeur than any other single one about the Valley. The Nevada and Vernal Falls are both plainly in sight, and directly over them is the Obelisk, with a portion of the range extending off to the right, until concealed behind the conical mass of Mount Starr King. To the left of the Cap of Liberty is the depression in which lies the Little Yosemite, and beyond this, in the farthest distance, the lofty summits of the Mount Lyell Group. The pines fringing the edge of Glacier Point are the *Pinus Jeffreyi*. The view of the Half Dome from this point is stupendous, as the

---

* Mount Lyell and Mount Maclure are two dark points visible to the right and the left of a snow-covered peak, rising in the farthest distance between the Nevada Fall and the Cap of Liberty.

spectator is very near to that object, and in a position to see it almost exactly edgewise. We regret that we are not able to give a figure of it from this point of view. Language is powerless to express the effect which this gigantic mass of rock, so utterly unlike anything else in the world, produces on the mind.

We have thus conducted the traveller around the Valley, and given him as many hints as our space will admit as to the character and locality of the objects to be seen on the route. A week is surely very little to devote to this excursion; and, when we consider how much can be seen and enjoyed during this time, it seems as if every one would be desirous of taking the opportunity of being at the Yosemite to make this addition to his travelling experience. The time will certainly come when this will be fully recognized, and when the rather indistinct trail around the Valley will be as well beaten as is now the one which leads into it.

For those who desire to extend their knowledge of the High Sierra still farther, there are numerous mountains, peaks, passes, and valleys to be visited, each one of which has its own peculiar beauties and attractions.

The Merced Group, which is so conspicuous an object in the view from Sentinel Dome and many other points about the Yosemite, offers a fine field for exploration. This group is a side-range, parallel with the main one, and about twelve miles from it. It runs from a point near the Little Yosemite, for about twelve miles, and then meets the transverse range coming from Mount Lyell and forming the divide between the San Joaquin and the Merced. Intersecting this, the Merced Group is continued to the southeast, and runs into a high peak, called Black Mountain; it then falls off, and becomes lost in the plateau which borders the San Joaquin.

At the northeast extremity of the group is the grand peak to which we first gave the name of the "Obelisk," from its peculiar shape, as seen from the region to the north of the Yosemite. It has, since that, been named Mount Clark, while the range to which it belongs is sometimes called the Obelisk Group, but, oftener, the Merced Group, because the branches of that river head around it. This is a noble range of mountains, with four conspicuous summits and many others of less prominence. The dominating peaks all lie at the intersection of spurs with the main range, as will be seen on the map. Mount Clark, or the Obelisk, is the one nearest the

Yosemite. All these peaks are nearly of the same height. The one next south of the Obelisk was called the Gray Peak, the next the Red Mountain, and the next Black Mountain, from the various colors which predominate on their upper portions. The last name had, however, been previously given to the highest point of the mass of ridges and peaks at the southern extremity of the range, south of the divide between the San Joaquin and the Merced. All these points, except Gray Peak, have been climbed by the Geological Survey, and they are all between 11,500 and 11,700 feet in elevation. Mount Clark was found to be an extremely sharp crest of granite, and was not climbed without considerable risk. Mr. King, who, with Mr. Gardner, made the ascent of the peak, says that its summit is so slender, that when on top of it they seemed to be suspended in the air.

An examination of the map will show how the spurs of the Merced Group break off in bold precipices to the north, with a more gradual descent to the south,—a peculiarity already mentioned as existing at the summit of Mount Hoffmann. The same is the case with the long crested ridge which forms the divide between the waters of the Merced and the San Joaquin. All these spurs and ridges open to the north with grand amphitheatres, where great glaciers once headed. The space enclosed between the Merced Group, the Mount Lyell Group, and the divide of the San Joaquin and Merced, forms a grand plateau about ten miles square, into which project the various spurs, coming down in parallel order, while in the centre there is a deep trough, sunk 2,000 feet below the general level, in which runs the Merced. The views from all the dominating points on the ridges surrounding this plateau are sublime, the region being one of the wildest and most inaccessible in the Sierra.

Our party, in charge of Mr. King, made an attempt to climb Mount Ritter, but, on account of the unfavorable weather, did not succeed in quite reaching the summit. They approached it from the southwest, passing to the south of Buena Vista Peak and Black Mountain. The Merced divide was found to be everywhere impassable for animals. Mr. King evidently considers Mount Ritter the culminating point of this portion of the Sierra, as he says that he climbed to a point about as high as Mount Dana, and had still above him an inaccessible peak some 400 or 500 feet high. To the south of this are some grand pinnacles of granite, very lofty and apparently inaccessible, to which we gave the name of "the Minarets." Our space is not sufficient to enable us to go into a description of this region; suffice it to say that there are here numerous peaks, yet unscaled and unnamed, to which the attention of mountain climbers is invited. Any one of them will furnish a panoramic view which will surely repay the lover of Alpine scenery for the expenditure of time and muscle required for its ascent.

There is a very interesting locality on the Tuolumne River, about sixteen miles from the Yosemite in a straight line, and in a direction a little west of north. It is called the Hetch-Hetchy Valley, an Indian name, the meaning of which we have been unable to ascertain. It is not only interesting on account of the beauty and grandeur of its scenery, but also because it is, in many respects, almost an exact counterpart of the Yosemite. It is not on quite so grand a scale as that valley; but, if there were no Yosemite, the Hetch-Hetchy would be fairly entitled to a world-wide fame; and, in spite of the superior attractions of the Yosemite, a visit to its counterpart may be recommended, if it be only to see how curiously Nature has repeated herself.

The Hetch-Hetchy may be reached easily from Big Oak Flat, by taking the regular Yosemite trail, by Sprague's ranch and Big Flume, as far as Mr. Hardin's fence, between the south and middle forks of the Tuolumne River. Here, at a distance of about eighteen miles from Big Oak Flat, the trail turns off to the left, going to Wade's meadows, or Big Meadows as they are also called, the distance being about seven miles. From Wade's ranch the trail crosses the middle fork of the Tuolumne, and goes to the "Hog ranch," a distance of five miles, then up the divide between the middle fork and the main river, to another little ranch called "the Cañon." From here, it winds down among the rocks for six miles, to the Hetch-Hetchy, or the Tuolumne Cañon. This trail was made by Mr. Joseph Screech, and is well blazed, and has been used for driving sheep and cattle into the Valley. The whole distance from Big Oak Flat is called thirty-eight miles. Mr. Screech first visited this place in 1850, at which time the Indians had possession. The Pah Utes still visit it every year for the purpose of getting the acorns, having driven out the western slope Indians, just as they did from the Yosemite.

The Hetch-Hetchy is between 3,800 and 3,900 feet above the sea-level, or nearly the same as the Yosemite; it is three miles long east and west, but is divided into two parts by a spur of granite, which nearly closes it up in the centre. The portion of the Valley below this spur is a large open meadow, a mile in length, and from an eighth to half a mile in width, with excellent grass, timbered only along the edge. The meadow terminates below in an extremely narrow cañon, through which the river has not sufficient room to flow at the time of the spring freshets, so that the Valley is then inundated, giving rise to a fine lake. The upper part of the Valley, east of the spur, is a mile and three quarters long, and from an eighth to a third of a mile wide, well timbered and grassed. The walls of this Valley are not quite so high as those of the Yosemite; but still, anywhere else than in California, they would be considered as wonderfully grand. On the north side of the Hetch-Hetchy is a perpendicular bluff, the edge of which is 1,800 feet above the Valley, and having a remarkable resemblance to El Capitan. In the spring, when the snows are melting, a large stream is precipitated over this cliff, falling at least 1,000 feet perpendicular. The volume of water is very large, and the whole of the lower part of the Valley is said to be filled with its spray.

A little farther east is the Hetch-Hetchy Fall, the counterpart of the Yosemite. The height is 1,700 feet. It is not quite perpendicular; but it comes down in a series of beautiful cascades, over a steeply-inclined face of rock. The volume of water is much larger than that of the Yosemite Fall, and, in the spring, its noise can be heard for miles. The position of this fall in relation to the Valley is exactly like that of the Yosemite Fall in its Valley, and opposite to it is a rock much resembling the Cathedral Rock, and 2,270 feet high.

At the upper end of the Valley the river forks, one branch, nearly as large as the main river, coming in from near Castle Peak. Above this, the cañon, so far as we know, is unexplored; but, in all probability, has concealed in it some grand falls. There is no doubt that the great glacier, which, as already mentioned, originated near Mount Dana and Mount Lyell, found its way down the Tuolumne Cañon, and passed through the Hetch-Hetchy Valley. How far beyond this it reached we are unable to say, for we have made no explorations in the cañon below. Within the Valley, the rocks are beautifully polished, up to at least 800 feet above the river. Indeed, it is probable that the glacier was much thicker than this; for, along, the trail, near the south end of the Hetch-Hetchy, a moraine was observed at the elevation of fully 1,200 feet above the bottom of the Valley. The great size and elevation of the amphitheatre in which the Tuolumne glacier headed caused such an immense mass of ice to be formed that it descended far below the line of perpetual snow before it melted away. The plateau, or amphitheatre, at the head of the Merced was not high enough to allow a glacier to be formed of sufficient thickness to descend down as far as into the Yosemite Valley; at least, we have obtained no positive evidence that such was the case. The statement to that effect in the "Geology of California," Vol. I., is an error, although it is certain that the masses of ice approached very near to the edge of the Valley, and were very thick in the cañon to the southeast of Cloud's Rest, and on down into the Little Yosemite.

This chapter may be closed by adding a few pages in regard to a portion of the High Sierra beyond the limits of the map accompanying this volume, but to which we desire to direct attention, as including the loftiest and the grandest mountains, and the most stupendous mountain scenery, yet discovered within our own territory.

By referring to the Table on page 39, it will be observed that between latitudes 36° and 37° there are peaks and passes higher than those described as existing near the Yosemite, there being a general rise of the mass of the Sierra as we go south. This high region, in which the passes exceed 12,000, and the peaks rise, in one instance at least, to 15,000 feet, lies at the head of King's and Kern Rivers and the San Joaquin. The most elevated peaks are between the parallels of 36° 30' and 37°, and are distant from the Yosemite, in a southeast direction, from 90 to 110 miles. This region was first explored by the Geological Survey in 1864, and a synopsis of the results of this reconnoissance will be found in the "Geology of California," Vol. I. (pp 365–402), from which some extracts will here be introduced, in the hope of attracting the attention of some travellers, who may thus be induced to push their explorations beyond the comparatively narrow limits of a trip to and around the Yosemite. The region in question is not very difficult of access; indeed, a very good idea of its grandeur may be obtained by only a short trip from Visalia and back.

Our party, consisting of Messrs. Brewer, Hoffmann, King, Gardner, and Cotter, took the field in May and proceeded from San Francisco across the plains of the San Joaquin to Visalia, from which point they entered the Sierra, ascending King's River to its source, and exploring the whole region about the head-waters of that and Kern River. Thence they made their way across the range by a pass over 12,000 feet high, passed up Owen's Valley, ascended the west branch of Owen's River, crossing the Sierra again at an altitude of 12,400 feet, and thence descending to the head of the San Joaquin River. The exploration was continued through the region of the head-waters of that stream and the Merced, connecting the reconnoissance with that of 1863 around the sources of the Tuolumne. The whole expedition occupied about three months, during which time the geography and geology of a district including an area of over 10,000 square miles were for the first time explored, the whole region having previously been entirely unknown. The results proved to be of the greatest interest, disclosing the fact that this was the highest part of the Sierra Nevada, which was something quite unexpected to most persons, Mount Shasta having long been considered the most elevated point in California.

Thomas's Saw-mill (Camp 164), at an elevation of 5,484 feet above the sea, and about forty miles northeast of Visalia, may be made the base of supplies for an expedition to this region. The mill stands on the edge of a beautiful meadow, the water from which runs into King's River. It is surrounded by a magnificent forest of the usual coniferous trees found in the Sierra at this altitude, and a little higher up the Big Trees (*Sequoia gigantea*) are abundant, as will be noticed in the next chapter.

A rocky summit, called Bald Mountain, about six miles east of Thomas's Mill, was ascended by our party for the purpose of getting the first idea of the topography of the unknown region about to be visited. It is easy of access, although 7,936 feet high, and offers a fine view of the neighboring country and the extended crest of the Sierra. Its position is at once seen to be on the great elevated divide between the waters of King's River on the north, and the Kaweah on the south. This divide runs up to the snowy mountains at the summit of the chain, and appeared to terminate in the highest group of peaks, some twenty-five or thirty miles distant. The ridge of the divide rises at intervals into peaks, each one commanding the country on either side and behind it, as well as forward to the east as far as the next high point in that direction. About eight or nine miles to the north, and several thousand feet below, is the cañon of King's River, which seems precipitous and impassable. Some twenty miles to the northeast this river divides into two branches, and the course of the northern of these is such that the observer on the summit of Bald Mountain can look directly into it. The view is most impressive. Granite walls with buttresses, pinnacles, and domes rise perpendicularly from three to five thousand feet above the river, and above these the bare, rocky slopes tower up, high above all vegetation into regions of perpetual snow. Dark lines of trees wind up the ravines on the mountain-sides, becoming thinner and more scattered, until they disappear altogether, the summits of the mountains rising far above all vegetation, barren and desolate.

Such is the character of the divide between the main forks of the King's River, although the southern side is not as steep as the northern. Its lofty summit, everywhere crested with precipices, presented an insurmountable barrier, over which our party never succeeded in taking their animals. Just at the junction of the forks, the end of the divide is crossed by a broad red stripe, bearing about northwest, and which could be seen appearing again on the north side of the cañon. This, which seemed to be a great dyke of volcanic rock, but which was afterwards found to be a vein of granite, led to giving the divide the name of "Dyke Ridge."

An attempt was first made to reach the summit of the Sierra by travelling up this divide, an old Indian trail being discovered which was followed for about fifteen miles. This trail led to a point where the ridge widened out into a plateau occupied by a large meadow; a number of cattle had been driven here, and the place was known to hunters as the "Big Meadows." Camp 165 was intermediate between Thomas's and the Big Meadows, and was 7,480 feet above the sea. The rock along the whole route is granite, which has a tendency to weather into grand, rounded, boulder-like masses. Camp 166, about two miles below the Big Meadows, but nearly at the same altitude, was at an elevation of 7,827 feet. Here the massive granite is traversed by occasional dykes of a fine-grained variety of the same rock, and with veins of milky quartz. Large areas of nearly level or gently-sloping ground occur here, covered with meadows or forests of *Pinus contorta*, and there are also extensive patches of bare rock, or of granitic sand derived from its decomposition. As the granite decomposes very irregularly, the harder portions rise in rocky, rounded hills, and the softer are occupied by small valleys. A series of these grassy plats, five or six miles in length, makes up the Big Meadows, and they are drained in both directions, namely, into the King's and Kaweah Rivers. At this altitude the sugar and pitch pines, as well as the Big Trees, are left behind, and the forests are made up of the dark and sombre fir and *Pinus contorta*. Although it was the month of June, the thermometer sank as low as 16° at night, and a snow-storm, of three or four hours' duration occurred.

Just east of the Big Meadows, and on the summit of the divide, are two elevations, to which the name of "Dome Mountains" was given, from the finely rounded, dome-like sweep of their outlines, which contrasts in a striking manner with the sharpness of the summit peaks behind them. On their southern sides the forests rise in an unbroken curve to their summits; but on the north side there is a precipice for 200 to 300 feet below the crest, then a short, concave curve, and then the rounded and wooded slope descending to the King's River Valley. In this part of the mountains, as at the Yosemite, the granite exhibits a tendency to form dome-shaped masses on a grand scale; but on the very crest or summit-range it rises in pinnacles, giving a very different character to the scenery, as will be noticed further on. That one of these Dome Mountains which was ascended was found to be 9,825 feet high. Its summit was made up of concentric layers or beds of granite, from one to five feet thick, breaking into large rectangular masses sufficiently smooth and regular in form to be used for masonry without dressing. The north slope of the mountain is covered by immense masses of this angular *débris*. That this concentric structure is not the result of the original stratification of the rock, is evident from a study of the phenomena, which do not indicate anything like anticlinal or synclinal axes, or any irregular folding. The curves are arranged strictly with reference to the surface of the masses of rock, showing clearly that they must have been produced by the contraction of the material while cooling or solidifying, and also giving very strongly the impression that, in many places, we see something of the original shape of the surface, as it was when the granitic mass assumed its present position. In the cañons between these domes, we sometimes have large surfaces exposed by denudation, and, as a result of the original concentric structure of the rocks on each side, we see the great plates of granite overlapping each other, and where considerable weathering and denudation has taken place, we have picturesque and curious forms as the result; pyramids and pinnacles are left standing on the prominent points, and their bedded structure adds to the peculiar impression which they give of their being works of art rather than of nature. Fig. 14 will serve to illustrate the kind of scenery which is common in the region of this concentrically bedded granite.

Fig. 14.

GRANITE ROCKS NEAR CAMP 169.

The route followed by the party, in their attempt to reach the summit, led around the north side of the Domes, over the huge piles of angular fragments, and was on this account tedious and difficult. Camp 167 was made at a point two miles northeast of the Dome, and at an altitude of 8,890 feet above the sea. Camp 168 was four or five miles southeast of the Dome, at a small meadow on the divide, and at an elevation of 9,569 feet. Progress was necessarily very slow, owing to the heavy load of provisions and instruments with which the small train of animals was packed, and the extreme roughness of the region travelled over. Beyond the Domes the divide contracts to a mere ridge; the slope to the south, although steep, is comparatively smooth, and spreads out, towards its base, into rolling wooded spurs, between which small brooks run down into the Kaweah. Nearly all these streams head in little sedgy meadows, whose bright green contrasts beautifully with the deep shade of the surrounding forests. To the north, the aspect of things was different; instead of a smooth slope, there was a fractured granite precipice, descending 200 feet, then a slope of *débris*, and at its foot two small lakes, forming the head-waters of a stream which unites with the south fork of King's River, a few miles above the dyke. This stream was called Glacier Brook, from the abundant traces of former glacial action in its vicinity. From Camp 168 to the Big Meadows is only sixteen miles; but so difficult was the way, that it required two days for the party to accomplish that distance. From this camp, and the next (No. 169), two miles farther up the divide, an examination was made of an interesting and characteristic feature in the topography of this granitic region, and to which the name of "The Kettle" was given.

This is a rocky amphitheatre at the head of a stream which flows back directly northeast from its source towards the axis of the chain, for a distance of twelve miles, and then curves and enters King's River, a peculiar and almost unique course for a stream in the Sierra Nevada. The kettle-like form of the head of this valley may be seen from the annexed section across

Fig. 15.

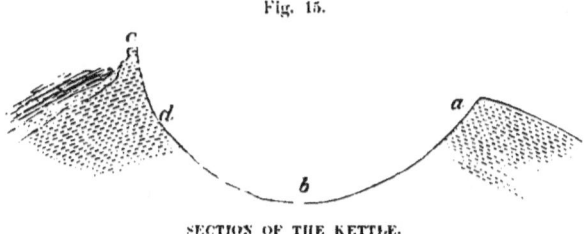

SECTION OF THE KETTLE.

it transversely, at a distance of about a mile from its head (Fig. 15): it is plotted on an equal scale of horizontal and vertical distances.

The northern rim (*a*) is about 1,100 feet above the bottom (*b*); the southern one (*c*) rises in a sharp ridge 1,606 feet above *b*; in some places *c d* is a vertical wall, in others a steep slope. The distance from *a* to *c* is a little less than a mile. The Kettle is open at the north-northeast end, and extends as a green valley some six miles, to the south fork of King's River. There are several small domes and pinnacles on the east side, and in some places the granite along the rim forms a parapet, which has a striking resemblance to an artificial structure, as the rock is most beautifully and regularly bedded, so that the wall seems to vie with the most finished mason-work in execution. The annexed woodcut (Fig. 16) will show the exact appearance of a portion of this wall, which is in some places so thin that the light can be seen shining through between the cracks. It is from eight to twenty feet high.

Fig. 16.

RIM OF THE KETTLE.

This rim of the Kettle is a beautiful illustration of the concentric or "dome-structure" of the granite of this region. The dotted lines in Fig. 15 show the bedding or lamination of the rock, in the cross-section of the whole, and Fig. 17 explains how the parapet has been formed by the wearing away of a part of the concentrically-laminated granite near the summit. This peculiar crater-like cavity in the granite is typical of many others seen afterwards in this region, the origin of which it seems impossible to refer to any ordinary denudation, or to the action of glaciers. These cavities were all occupied by masses of ice, as is evident from the polish of the interior walls and bottom of each of them; but it hardly needs to be added that no glacial action could have originally formed one of these kettles; the most that it could do would be to scour out and polish up the interior. This subject will be discussed in the second volume of the "Geology of California."

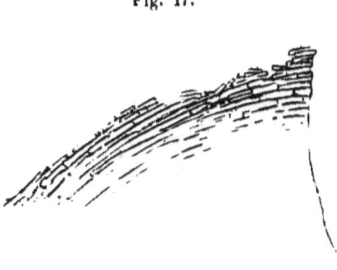

Fig. 17.

Beyond the Kettle the divide becomes quite impassable for animals, and nearly so for men. Several unsuccessful trials were made to pass the barrier of nearly perpendicular rocks; but, at last, a chink in the granite was found, through which the party crawled, and proceeded to ascend the next high peak on the divide, which is about six miles southeast of Camp 169, the elevation of which was found to be 11,623 feet above the sea. From its summit a magnificent view was obtained of the crest of the Sierra, as well as of the divide which had been traversed by the party. The region to the east presented a complicated system of very sharp ridges, rising here and there into pinnacles, apparently all of granite, with numerous immense circular amphitheatral cavities, formed by sharp ridges surrounding basins, of which one side is always broken away, and which have exactly the appearance of ancient craters both in form and outline. To the west the predominance of rounded or dome-shaped mountain summits was most striking, the whole country appearing as if it had suddenly been cooled or congealed while violently boiling.

Camp 170 was about seven miles north-northeast of No. 169, in the valley of the stream which flows from the Kettle, and at an altitude of 7,408 feet, which was a lower point than was afterwards reached by the party for a long time. The way to this camp led around the west and north sides of the Kettle over a region exceedingly difficult to traverse, with alternating steep, naked slopes of granite, and thick, low forests. Some of the ancient moraines, piles of angular fragments of granite, were almost insurmountable obstacles to the passage of the animals. This camp was situated behind a sharp granite knob which rises from the valley like a sugar-loaf, as seen from below; but which, in reality, is the end of a ridge a mile or two in length. This is several hundred feet high, and its summit is quite inaccessible. Its sides show undoubted evidence that it was once surrounded by a great glacier flowing down the valley. The slopes directed towards the moving ice are worn and polished, and huge boulders have been pushed up on them, and left all along, wherever the angle was not too steep for fragments of rock to lie. The meadow occupies a basin behind this knob, which appears to have been scooped out by a glacier.

From the Sugar Loaf Rock there is a magnificent view up the valley to the group of mountains forming the western crest of the Sierra, the culminating point of which was named Mount Brewer. This was directly east, and about ten miles distant. A grand view was also had of the great moraine on the eastern side of the extreme south fork of King's River; this moraine stretches along for six or eight miles in an unbroken line, resembling an immense artificial embankment. There is another one on the opposite side of the valley which is also very distinct, but the eastern one is much the larger. The horizontal distance across from one to the other is about a mile and a half. At a distance these moraines appear as regular as railroad embankments, their crests being quite smooth, and having a uniform and gradual inclination up the valley. To ascend or descend their sides with animals, is a task of considerable difficulty; but, once on the top, travelling is quite easy. In the bottom of the valley the granite is everywhere grooved and beautifully polished.

The view of the cañon, towards its head, as seen from this moraine, near Camp 175, was sublime, strongly resembling the valley of the Yosemite in some of its grandest features. It curves but little, so that the view is unobstructed. Great surfaces and precipices of naked granite are seen, often over 1,000 feet high, but seldom vertical, although sloping at a very high angle; these surfaces are everywhere in the valley rounded and polished. Side cañons of the same character, but still more precipitous, open into the main one.

From Camp 171, Mount Brewer was twice ascended, on the 2d and 4th of July, by passing up the valley in which the camp was situated, and which divides at the base of the mountain, extending up to the crest of the ridge. Its sides were found to be very steep up to above 12,000 feet, the southern one being an almost vertical wall of 1,000 feet in height. The granite of this region is hard, not very coarse, and of a light ash-gray color, with a pearly lustre when seen in great masses. It is intersected with veins

Fig. 18.

MOUNT BREWER, FROM A POINT THREE MILES DISTANT, LOOKING EAST.

of quartz and also of feldspar, and with some made up of a mixture of both these minerals; these veins were rarely more than two or three feet in thickness. In general, however, the rock is remarkably homogeneous and almost destitute of accidental minerals, a little epidote being the only one observed in this region.

The view from the summit of Mount Brewer is one of the most sublime which it is possible to obtain, even in this sublimest portion of the Sierra. The snowy peaks, rising to over 11,000 feet in elevation, cover a breadth of more than twenty-five miles, and the point of view on the summit of this mountain is such, that the observer is placed in the very midst of this grand assemblage. High peaks, sharp ridges bristling with pinnacles, rocky amphitheatres, and deep cañons constitute the main features of the scene. The summit is a loose and shattered mass of angular pieces of granite, forming a ridge some thirty feet long by five broad, which from the west appears as a sharp cone. The eastern side of the mountain is a precipice buttressed by a thin ridge, running out between two great vertically-walled basins, white with snow, which contrasts beautifully with the vivid blue of the frozen lakes 3,000 feet below.

The barometrical measurements make the height of Mount Brewer 13,886 feet; it is not, however, the culminating point of the Sierra, but is on a spur embraced by two branches of King's River. Ten miles farther east another ridge stretches in an unbroken line north and south, and through its depressions the blue ranges of the desert are plainly seen. On this ridge there are fourteen peaks visible, ten of which are as high as Mount Brewer, and four higher. One of these, directly opposite, and which appeared to be the highest point but one, was called Mount Tyndall, in honor of this distinguished physicist and Alpine explorer. The other high point, eight miles south of Mount Tyndall, and, so far as known, the culminating peak of the Sierra, was named by the party Mount Whitney. Farther observations, by Mr. King, showed that a point about two miles northeast of Mount Tyndall was a little higher than this mountain; it was named in honor of Major R. S. Williamson, of the United States Engineers, so well known by his topographical labors on the Pacific coast, especially in connection with the United States railroad surveys. Thirty-two miles north-northwest is a very high mountain, called Mount Goddard, in honor of a Civil Engineer who has done much to advance our knowledge of the geography of California, and who is the author of "Britton and Rey's Map." A transverse ridge running obliquely across from Mount Brewer to Mount Tyndall forms the divide between the head-waters of the Kern and those of King's River. South of this, the division of the summit of the Sierra into two parallel ridges is very marked, the Kern flowing in the tremendous gorge between them. The eastern ridge forms an almost unbroken wall for a great distance to the north, while the western one is less distinctly marked, being broken through to allow of the passage of the head-waters of the King's and San Joaquin Rivers. The highest portion of the western ridge is that extending between Mount Brewer and Kaweah Peak, twelve miles to the south. This last-named peak was not reached by our party, but its height was estimated to be over 14,000 feet. From its great elevation and peculiar position, opposite to the highest point of the Sierra, and the immense depth of the cañon of the Kern between it and Mount Whitney, it would probably command the grandest view which could be obtained in the whole range of the Sierra. Kaweah Peak is distinctly visible from Visalia, to one looking up the valley of the Kaweah River.

Of the terrible grandeur of the region embraced in this portion of the Sierra it is hardly possible to convey any idea. Mr. Gardner, in his notes of the view from Mount Brewer, thus enumerates some of the most striking features of the scene: "Cañons from two to five thousand feet deep, between thin ridges topped with pinnacles sharp as needles; successions of great, crater-like amphitheatres, with crowning precipices over sweeping snow-fields and frozen lakes; everywhere naked and shattered granite without a sign of vegetation, except where a few gnarled and storm-beaten pines (*Pinus contorta*, *P. albicaulis*, and *P. aristata*) cling to the rocks in the deeper cañons; such were the elements of the scene we looked down upon, while cold gray clouds were drifting overhead."

The upper part of the mountain slopes rapidly on all sides for 2,000 feet from the summit, then falls off more gradually on the west towards the cañon of the south fork of King's River. On the east, it breaks off suddenly into a great amphitheatre, the head of a cañon between 4,000 and 5,000 feet deep below the crest, surrounded by sheer vertical walls, and with glacier-polished slopes at the bottom, over which are scattered several small and beautiful lakes. These cañons and precipices, which lie between the two principal ridges, constitute the main difficulty in reaching and exploring the eastern summit peaks. The region is desolate and cold; but these hindrances, incidental to all high mountain climbing, could be overcome, were it not for the impassable precipices which continually block the way, necessitating long *détours*, and rendering it impossible to reach any high peak without a long series of perilous and extremely fatiguing ascents and descents.

As want of provisions and the absolute impossibility of proceeding any farther with the animals were sufficient reasons to prevent the whole party from making any attempt to climb the summit of the eastern ridge, Mr. King volunteered to undertake this task, although it seemed to most of the party that it was quite impossible to reach either of the highest peaks from the western side. Packing provisions for six days and one blanket, he started, accompanied by Richard Cotter, from the camp at the base of Mount Brewer, July 4th, and the following account of the trip, in which the summit of Mount Tyndall was reached, is given nearly in Mr. King's own words:—

"To follow down the ridge which forms the divide between King's and Kern Rivers, and which runs obliquely across from Mount Brewer to Mount Tyndall, was impossible, for it rose in sharp crags above us, and had we been able to pass around these, we should have been stopped by vertical clefts over a thousand feet deep. We began, therefore, to climb down the eastern slope of the ridge, instead of trying to keep on its crest. The only way down was along a sloping shelf, on which we were obliged to proceed with the greatest caution, as our packs had a constant tendency to overbalance us, and a single misstep would have been fatal. At last we reached the base of the cliff safely, and made our way rapidly down a long snow-slope and over huge angular masses of *débris* to the margin of a frozen lake.

"We were now in the amphitheatre; the crags towering around us were all inaccessible, and we were obliged to spend six hours in climbing down from the outlet of the lake, over a slope of smooth granite, polished by glaciers and kept constantly wet by a shallow current of water, into King's River cañon, and then up again over a long, difficult *débris* slope and across several fields of snow, into another amphitheatre. Of this the southern wall is the divide between King's and Kern Rivers. The sky by this time had become quite overcast, and we were obliged to take refuge under some overhanging rocks, while a severe hail-storm went by. We started on again, hoping to cross over to Kern Cañon; but the ascent proved very difficult, and night overtook us at the foot of a cliff 2,000 feet high. There was no wood, so we burned paper and dead carices enough to make some lukewarm tea, and finding a crevice among the ice and granite blocks, somewhat sheltered from the biting winds, we retired. The elevation was over 12,000 feet, and the air stinging cold; but the sunset view was glorious. The east wall of the basin was brilliantly lighted up, its hundred pinnacles were of pure yellow, relieved by the dark blue of the sky, which is so noticeable when one looks up from a deep cañon in the Sierra. A long slope of snow opposite us warmed with a soft rosy tinge (the Alpine glow), and the rugged ridge behind us cast a serrated gray shadow across it, which slowly crept up and scaled the granite wall, until only the very topmost spires were in the light. All night long, large masses of granite came crashing down from the crags overhead, striking at times too near for comfort.

"The next morning we ate our frozen venison by starlight, and started at sunrise to ascend the snow-slope before it should become softened. We had to cut steps, and after working up awhile it became quite difficult, so that we were three hours in reaching the rocks, after which we climbed two hours more, until we came to a very bad ravine where it was impossible to proceed with our packs. It was now that our reata came into play, and we took turns in climbing the length of it, and pulling packs and blankets after us, reaching the top about noon, by which time the novelty of this method of ascent had quite worn off. What was our consternation to find ourselves, as we scaled the summit, on the brink of an almost Yosemite cliff! We walked along the edge, however, for some distance, until at last we discovered three shelves, each about fifty feet below the other, from the lowest of which we might, by good luck and hard climbing, work along the face of the cliff to a sort of ravine, down which we might probably reach the *débris*. I tied the reata firmly about my body, and Cotter lowered me down to the first shelf; he then carefully sent down the precious barometer and our packs. Next, he made a fast loop in the lasso, hooked it over a point of rock and came down hand over hand, whipping the rope off the rock to which it had been fastened, thus severing our communication with the top of the cliff. This operation was repeated, not without considerable danger, from the impossibility of finding a firm rock around which to secure the rope, until the bottom was at last safely reached. At the foot of the *débris* was a beautiful lake half a mile long, once the bottom of the bed of a glacier.

"There were a few *Pinus contorta* visible down the course of the Kern, — here only a small brook, — and quite a grove of *P. aristata*; these, with a few willows and an Alpine *Ribes*, were all the vegetation we could see, excepting a few carices. Camp was made at the base of the peak, after climbing up a difficult ridge, near a little cluster of the *Pinus contorta*; this was about 11,000 feet above the sea.

"The next day the summit was reached, without serious difficulty, after some risky climbing of smooth dome-shaped masses of granite, where the only support and aid in climbing was an occasional crack. The barometer stood, at 12 M., at 18,104, the temperature of the air being 44°. On setting the level, it was seen at once that there were two peaks equally high in sight, and two still more elevated, all within a distance of seven miles. Of the two highest, one rose close by, hardly a mile away; it is an inaccessible bunch of needles, and we gave it the name of Mount Williamson. The other, which we called Mount Whitney, appeared equally inaccessible from any point on the north or west side; it is between seven and eight miles distant, in a south-southeast direction, and I should think fully 350 feet higher than our peak. (Farther examination showed that it was really 600 or 700 feet higher than Mount Tyndall.) Within our field of view were five mountains over 14,000 feet, and about fifty peaks over 13,000.

"The five highest peaks are all on the eastern ridge. Owen's Valley, a brown sage plain, lies 10,000 feet below on the one side, and Kern Cañon, once the rocky bed of a grand old glacier, 4,000 feet down on the other. About fifteen miles north of here, King's River cuts through the western ridge and turns at a right angle towards the plain. North of this point, again, the two great ridges unite in a grand pile of granite mountains, whose outlines are all of the most rugged and fantastic character. Twenty-five miles south, the high group ends, there (certainly for a breadth of sixty miles) forming one broad, rolling, forest-covered plateau, 8,000 to 9,000 feet in elevation.

"From Mount Brewer to Kaweah Peak, the two culminating points of the western ridge, for a distance of fifteen miles, there is nothing that can be called a separate mountain; it is, rather, a great mural ridge, capped by small, sharp cones and low, rugged domes, all covered with little minarets. At one place the ridge forms a level table; upon this lies an unbroken cover of snow. To the eastward, all this range, from King's River gateway to Kaweah Peak, presents a series of blank, almost perpendicular precipices, broken every mile or so by a bold granite buttress. Between these are vast snow-fields, and also numberless deep lakes, of which the most elevated are frozen."

The elevation of Mount Tyndall, as calculated from Mr. King's observations, compared with those of the other party, and with the station barometer at Visalia, was fixed at 14,386 feet; this is only fifty-four feet less than the altitude of Mount Shasta.

After Mr. King's return to Camp 171, at the eastern base of Mount Brewer, the whole party went back to Big Meadows, having been out of provisions for several days, with the exception of a few strips of jerked bear meat. Here, also, they were to meet the escort which was considered indispensable for safely exploring the region to the north. Mr. King, however, not being satisfied with his first attempt to reach the culminating point of the Sierra, made another start from Visalia July 14th, with no other company than an escort of two soldiers. His intention was to follow the Owen's Lake and Visalia trail, which leads up the Kaweah River, keeping the south fork from its junction with the main river. It was supposed that it might be possible to reach the summit of Mount Whitney from this side, previous explorations having shown that this could not be accomplished from the northwest or west.

The first camp was at forty miles distance from the edge of the foot-hills, the road up the valley being intensely hot, dry, and dusty. From this camp the trail led over a rolling plateau of high altitude (probably between 8,000 and 9,000 feet), partly covered by forests of *Pinus contorta*, and partly by chains of meadows. North of the road was a range of bald, granite hills, with groves of pine scattered about their bases, an occasional patch of snow appearing on the higher points. This chain of peaks seems to be the continuation of the divide between the south and main Kaweah Rivers, and it continues eastward to the summit of the Sierra, being the southern termination of the high ranges to the north; south of it the country falls off gradually to Walker's Pass, forming numerous broad, flat-topped ridges, which give the region the general aspect of a table-land, scored down from north to south by parallel cañons, of which the Kern occupies the deepest. The main and north forks of this river rise far to the north of this tableland, and cut their way through it, while the south fork heads on its southern slope, and joins the main river, about eight miles below where the trail crosses. This plateau is entirely of granite, and the vegetation varies according to the altitude. West of the cañon of the south fork, the forests are chiefly of the *Pinus contorta;* between this and the main Kern are fine groves of *P. Jeffreyi,* and occasional oaks. Where the trail crosses the main Kern, the river is twenty-five or thirty yards wide; the water is clear and cold, and abundantly supplied with trout.

From this point the old trail bent southward, crossing the mountains some distance below Little Owen's Lake; the new one was built no farther, and from here it was necessary to continue the exploration, without any other guides than the eye and the compass. Striking the north fork of the Kern, at that point only a brook four or five yards wide, Mr. King followed it up for several miles, to where it breaks through an east and west range of craggy peaks, which comes down like an immense spur, at right-angles to the general course of the Sierra, and is continued as an elevated ridge far down the north side of the Kaweah. This range heads in a very high and bare granitic peak, called Sheep Rock, from the great number of mountain sheep found in this vicinity. It is about eight miles south of Mount Whitney, and is the termination of this high portion of the Sierra.

North of this spur or lateral range through which the north and main forks of the Kern both make their way, there is a quadrilateral area, comprised between the two great divisions of the Sierra on the east and west sides, and having on the north the transverse ridge which connects Mount Tyndall with Mount Whitney. In this the main Kern heads with many branches, and to the east of it, in the midst of every difficulty, Mr. King worked for three days before he could reach the base of the mountain, whose summit he was endeavoring to attain. All his efforts, however, proved unsuccessful, so far as this particular object was concerned; but he was enabled to determine the main features of the topography of a considerable area, which otherwise would necessarily have been left an entire blank upon our map. The highest point reached by him was, according to the most reliable calculations, 14,740 feet above the sea-level. At the place where this observation was taken he was, as near as he was able to estimate, between 300 and 400 feet lower than the culminating point of the mountain, which must, therefore, somewhat exceed 15,000 feet in height.

The summit is a ridge having somewhat the outline of a helmet, the perpendicular face being turned towards the east, and there is snow on its summit, which indicates that there must be a flat surface there. It is the culminating point of an immense pile of granite, which is cut almost to the centre by numerous steep and often almost vertical cañons, ending in high-walled amphitheatres. Southward of the main peak there is a range of sharp needles, four of which are over 14,000 feet high. The general aspect of the group is much like that of Mount Tyndall. Mount Whitney has been approached on all sides, except from the east, and, so far, found to be utterly inaccessible.

During the time while Mr. King was exploring about the sources of Kern River, Professor Brewer and party continued their route northward, in the hope of being able to cross over the higher ridges of the Sierra to the head of the San Joaquin. They left the Big Meadows and made their way into the great cañon of the south fork of King's River by a terribly steep road, the descent being between 4,500 and 5,000 feet. The cañon here is very much like the Yosemite. It is a valley, from half a mile to a mile wide at the bottom, about eleven miles long, and closed at the lower end by a deep and inaccessible ravine like that below the Yosemite, but deeper and more precipitous. It expands above and branches at its head, and is everywhere surrounded and walled in by grand precipices, broken here and there by side cañons, resembling the Yosemite in its main features. The walls of the King's River cañon, however, are nowhere vertical to so great a height as El Capitan; but rather resemble the Sentinel and Cathedral Rocks, or the Three Brothers, of the Yosemite Valley. They rise at various points to heights estimated to be from 3,500 to 6,000 feet above their base, and there is but little *débris* at the foot of the walls. The height of the lower end of the valley above the sea was found to be approximately 4,737 feet; that of the upper end, 5,218 feet. At the head of the valley, occupying a position analogous to that of the Half Dome at the Yosemite, is the most elevated part of the wall; it is nearly vertical, and between 6,500 and 7,000 feet high.

The King's River cañon rivals and even surpasses the Yosemite Valley in the altitude of its surrounding cliffs; but it has no features so striking as the Half Dome, or Tutucanula, nor has it the stupendous waterfalls which make that valley quite unrivalled in beauty; its streams descend by a series of what may be called (in California) cascades, of from 150 to 200 feet high.

The bottom of the valley is covered with granitic sand, forming a soil which supports a fine growth of timber, with here and there a meadow. The river abounds in trout.

The party came into the valley by an old Indian foot-trail, which passes out by the north fork, over an exceedingly rough country, and must cross the Sierra at an elevation of at least 13,000 feet. This trail was entirely impracticable for animals. As it was quite impossible to get north at the head of the valley, the party returned a distance of two or three miles, and made their way out on the north side, by an exceedingly steep and difficult route, camping four or five miles from the edge of the cañon, and at an elevation of more than 4,000 feet above it, or 9,308 feet above the sea. This camp (No. 180) was situated between the two main forks of King's River, and from it a series of fruitless attempts were made to reach Mount Goddard, about twenty-four miles distant, in a north-northwesterly direction. The ridge between the forks of the King's rises up in a crest, which, three miles southwest of Camp 180, is 12,400 feet above the sea. From the summit of this ridge there is a precipitous descent to the north, into the cañon of the middle fork, which is, perhaps, even deeper than the one just described.

The crest presents a very serrated outline. Two peaks lying just in front of it are especially fine: they are between five and six miles east of Camp 180; both are probably over 14,000 feet high, the northern being a little the higher. This was named Mount King, and the southern one Mount Gardner. Mount King breaks off in grand precipices on the northwest side, like the Half Dome: these are several thousand feet in height, and almost vertical, producing the effect of an immense obelisk. The annexed woodcut (Fig. 19), from a sketch by Mr. Hoffmann, gives an idea of the form of this grand peak; the point of view was at Camp 180, about six miles west of the summit.

The region around the crest of the ridge between the forks of the King's

Fig. 19.

MOUNT KING, LOOKING EAST, FROM CAMP 180.

consists of granite masses, with spurs projecting out from them, and embracing basins of bare rock, each having a small lake at the bottom. The only living things visible in these valleys are the grasses in the small meadows which border the lakes. Everywhere else are to be seen only smooth, bare rocks, or granitic *débris* in steeply-sloping piles at the base of the precipices. The crests of the ridges are thin and shattered, — so thin that, in some cases, they could only be traversed by hitching the body over while sitting astride of them.

At the head of the north fork, along the main crest of the Sierra, is a range of peaks, from 13,500 to 14,000 feet high, which we called "the Palisades." These were unlike the rest of the crest in outline and color, and were doubtless volcanic; they were very grand and fantastic in shape, like the rocks seen on the Silver Mountain trail near Ebbett's Pass. (See Plate III.) All doubts as to the nature of these peaks were removed after observing on the east side of the crest, in Owen's Valley, vast streams of lava which had flowed down the slope of the Sierra, just below the Palisades.

Three days were spent by the party in trying to find some place where the ridge between the forks of the King's could be crossed with animals, so that the party could reach the middle fork and thence make their way to Mount Goddard. This was ascertained to be impossible, and it was found necessary to return to the cañon of the south fork. From here it was, after some hesitation, decided to cross the mountains into Owen's Valley, and, after following it up for forty or fifty miles, to turn west and cross the Sierra again, so as thus to reach the head-waters of the San Joaquin, over a trail which was made, in 1863, by a party of soldiers in pursuit of Indians.

A day and a half was required to make the distance of twelve miles which lay between Camp 179, in the south fork cañon, and the summit of the Sierra; although the labor of crossing was much facilitated by the fact that a party of prospectors had crossed here not long before, and had done a good deal towards making a passable trail. Camp 181, midway between the valley and the summit, was found to be 9,627 feet high. To the north of this camp, and nearly east of Mount King, but on the main crest of the Sierra, was a high, naked rock, rising fully 3,000 feet above the trail at its base, and one of the grandest objects seen among these mountains. The sketch (Fig. 20) will serve to convey a faint idea of its majestic form.

The distance from Camp 181 to the summit was found to be about eight miles. The crest, on the pass, is double, the first summit being 11,031 feet high, and the eastern one 12,057 feet. The latter is a very sharp ridge, with both sides inclined at as steep an angle as the loose materials could maintain without sliding; the actual crest is a sharp comb of rock. The peaks on each side are very steep, and were estimated to be 2,500 feet above the pass, or fully 14,500 feet above the sea. At this time (July 27) there was no snow on the line traversed by our party, although large patches were seen much lower down in shaded localities.

From the crest of the Sierra to its base in Owen's Valley is about eight miles in a direct line, and the average descent is just 1,000 feet per mile for that distance. From the foot of the mountains a gradual and uniform slope extends into the valley, forming an inclined plane, strewn with boulders resting upon a sandy soil. This plain is dry and barren, and covered with the usual desert shrubs, Artemisia, Purshia, Linosyris, and others. The

Fig. 20.

PEAK NEAR CAMP 181.

highest peaks of the main crest are not more than ten or eleven miles from the valley, and fully 10,500 feet above it.

The mountains were entered again at the head of the west branch of Owen's River, on which Camp 187 was situated, at an elevation of 9,298 feet above the sea. To the north of this is an extremely barren table of lava, and on the south granite. The valley of the stream is half a mile wide, and flanked on both sides by beautifully regular moraines, from 1,000 to 1,200 feet above the bottom.

The summit of the Sierra was crossed at an altitude of 12,400 feet, and although the crest rose up in front, appearing as one continuous wall, and seemingly not to be scaled, yet the ascent was found to be on a comparatively easy grade, with the exception of one rocky place near the summit. There is an obscure Indian foot-trail which crosses here, and a body of seventy cavalry, with their pack-train, crossed by it in June, 1863. At that time there were patches of snow half a mile long upon the road. A wagon road could be made over this pass, without much difficulty; but its great height, and the immense body of snow which must lie here during nearly or quite all the year, forbid the idea of any such undertaking. The crest here is very rugged, rising in precipitous ridges about 1,000 feet above the pass in its immediate vicinity, and perhaps 2,000 feet at a little distance north and south.

The views from the high points above the trail at the summit were of the grandest description. Eight miles to the north was a group of dark, crimson-colored peaks, and twenty-five miles farther in that direction were the snow-clad ranges near Mono Lake. In a southerly direction rose a vast mass of granite peaks and ridges, with the same sharp scattered crests, vertical cliffs overhanging snow-fields and amphitheatres with frozen lakes, which were the main features of the views in the region about the head of King's River.

On the west side of the pass there was one mile of rocky and steep descent; but otherwise no difficulty was experienced. Great slopes were traversed, which were worn and polished by glaciers, and, as everywhere else in the Sierra, these exhibitions of ancient glacial phenomena were exhibited on a much grander scale on the west slope of the Sierra than they had been observed to be on the eastern side.

Camp 188, a little below the summit, was at an elevation of 9,940 feet, and from this high peaks on both sides were ascended and examined. Mr. Gardner visited the crimson-colored group noticed above, and which was about five miles north of the camp. The rocks were found to be of metamorphic slate, which continues about eight miles to the north, and is there lost under the granite. Enclosed in the slate, and having the same dip and strike, is a vein of white quartz rock sixty to seventy feet wide. The "Red Slate Peaks," as they were called, were found to be about 13,400 feet in elevation. This group forms the northern termination of the great elevated range of the Sierra, which stretches to the south, for a distance of over ninety miles, without any depression below 12,000 feet, in all probability the highest continuous mass of mountains in North America. To the north, between the Red Slate Peaks and the Mono Group, a considerable depression exists, over which is a pass, of the height of which we have no positive knowledge.

There is a great depression where the three largest branches of the King's come together. In this Camp 189 was made, at a distance of twenty-two miles from the summit of the Sierra, and 6,930 feet above the sea. Grassy meadows occur here, and rising above them are many rocky knolls rounded by former glaciers. This locality has long been a favorite resort of the Indians, on account of its remoteness from the settled part of California, and its consequent security. The abundance of game and the great number of pine trees in this valley also added to its charms. Thousands of trees were seen which had trenches dug around them, to catch the worms which live in the bark, as is said; these, as well as the nuts of the pine, are staple articles of food among the "Diggers." All the movements of our party were watched by the Indians from a distance and signalled by smokes, but no attack was made, as there might have been, had they not been provided with an escort.

From Camp 189 the country to the south was explored, in the direction of Mount Goddard, an important topographical station for connecting with the work on the other side of the King's. In going from Camp 189 to 190 the middle and south forks of the San Joaquin were crossed, and a due south course was kept towards a high point on the ridge, eight miles distant. The valley widens out here, and includes a broad belt of rolling country, with numerous low hills of granite, whose tops and sides are all smoothly rounded by glacial action. The predominant trees here are *Pinus Jeffreyi* and *P. contorta*. As we rise out of the valley, immense moraines are seen at the height of from 1,500 to 2,000 feet above the valley. A glacier, at least 1,500 feet deep, eight or nine miles wide, and probably thirty miles long, perhaps much more, once flowed down this valley, and has left its traces everywhere along its sides.

A peak a little south of Camp 190, and 10,711 feet above the sea, was climbed; from this a grand view of the Sierra between the Obelisk Range and the Mount Brewer Group was obtained. The snow lay on this ridge several hundred feet below the summit; but the *Pinus albicaulis* grows to the very top. This forms one of a series of high points which extend in a line nearly parallel with the crest of the Sierra, and from sixteen to twenty miles distant from it, thus preserving all through this region the same double-crested character which the range has farther south around the head of King's River.

The next move took the party about twelve miles in a southeasterly direction, and to a point only eighteen miles from Mount Goddard. This camp (No. 191) was at an elevation of 10,268 feet. The route followed lay along and over a ridge, with a very sharp crest breaking off in grand precipices on each side. It has also a parapet along the south edge similar to that described as forming the rim of the Kettle; this is in places thirty feet high, and rises like a grand wall, with a narrow shelf on the north; from this there is a very steep slope down for a thousand feet or more.

From Camp 191 an unsuccessful attempt was made to reach Mount Goddard, without the animals, as they could be taken no farther. The only possible way led along the divide between King's and San Joaquin Rivers, over a series of ridges, high and sharp, with valleys between, a thousand feet deep or more, so that progress was excessively slow and tiresome. Cotter and one of the soldiers succeeded, after a day's climbing, in getting within 300 feet of the summit, and hung up the barometer just before it was too dark to see to read it. They were then at an elevation of 13,648 feet, making the height of the mountain about 14,000 feet. The return to an impromptu camp, at an elevation of about 12,000 feet and without provisions or fire, made by the remainder of the party at the base of the mountain, required the whole night, and was hazardous in the extreme.

From Camp 191 the party returned to 189, and from there worked to the northwest in the cañon of the north fork of the San Joaquin. For three fourths of the way the route followed led down the depression at the junction of the three forks before noticed. This depression has the appearance of a valley only when seen from the heights around it. There are numerous flats lying between rounded hills of bare granite; these flats are sometimes covered by forests, but many of them form beautiful open meadows in which many thousand cattle might be pastured.

The north fork of the San Joaquin comes down through a very deep cañon, and the wide, open, valley-like depression terminates here. This cañon is from 3,000 to 4,000 feet deep, and proved to be a serious obstacle to the advance of the party. Near the junction of the north and main forks it is a mere notch, and its walls exhibit some grandly picturesque features. Two or three miles southeast of this is a most remarkable dome, more perfect in its form than any before seen in the State. It rises to the height of 1,800 feet above the river, and presents exactly the appearance of the upper part of a sphere; or, as Professor Brewer says, "of the top of a gigantic balloon struggling to get up through the rock."

Camp 194, in the cañon, was at an altitude of about 4,750 feet, while the ranges to the east and northeast rose from 4,000 to 5,000 feet above this, and those on the west about 3,000 feet. The sides of the cañon are very abrupt, and present immense surfaces of naked granite, resembling the valley of the Yosemite. There are everywhere in this valley the traces of former glaciers, on an immense scale, and as the party rose above the cañon on the north, in leaving the river, the moraine on the opposite side was seen very distinctly, and appeared to be at an elevation of not less than 3,000 feet above the bottom of the valley. It was evident that the glaciers which came down the various branches of the San Joaquin all united here to form one immense "sea of ice," which filled the whole of the wide depression spoken of above, and left its moraines at this high elevation above the present river-bed.

The party passed out of the cañon to the northwest, first ascending a steep ridge, over 3,000 feet high, and then entering a wide elevated valley, where Camp 195 was made, at an elevation of about 7,250 feet. On the high ridge traversed in getting to this camp were many boulders of lava, which must have been brought from some more northerly point and dropped in their present position by ancient glaciers. The source of these boulders seems to have been near Mount Clark, in the Obelisk Range. The view from the summit of the ridge was a grand one, commanding the whole of the Mount Lyell and Obelisk Groups, as well as the main range of the Sierra to the east, where are many dark-colored peaks, apparently volcanic. A very high and massive peak was seen to the east of Mount Lyell, which has since been named by us Mount Ritter, and is believed to be the dominating point of the group (see page 109).

In the depression to the west of the ridge noticed above are heavy forests and fine meadows scattered over the country, into which many cattle had been driven from Fresno County, to escape the extreme drought of the season. The meadows occupy the flats or level intervals between the domes of granite; grassy "flats," as they are called, occur everywhere along the Sierra at about this altitude, on the high lands between the large streams.

Camp 196, a few miles north of 195, was at the base of a prominent peak, which was supposed to belong to the Obelisk Group, for which the party was aiming. On ascending it, however, it was found to be about ten miles due south of the Obelisk. It was found to be 10,950 feet high and commanded a fine view. This is called Black Mountain on the map accompanying the present volume. Eighteen miles northeast of this is the lowest gap or pass over the Sierra which occurs between Carson's and Walker's Passes, a distance of about 250 miles. An approximation to its height was obtained by an observation of the barometer on the peak ascended near Camp 195, at a point which was ascertained by levelling to be at about the same altitude as the pass itself. The result of the calculation gave 9,200 feet as the height of the summit of the pass, which is considerably lower than the Mono Pass. Cattle have been driven across to Owen's Valley over this route, the north fork of the San Joaquin being crossed at a point much farther up than where our party traversed it, and where the cañon is not nearly so deep.

From Camp 196 the party made their way, as rapidly as the worn-out condition of the men and horses permitted, to Clark's ranch, on the trail from Mariposa to the Yosemite. They first travelled in a southwesterly direction, over a region of dome-shaped granite hills, for a distance of twenty-three miles, and camped at the head of the Chiquito San Joaquin, and at the altitude of 7,463 feet. Many meadows were passed, into which large numbers of cattle had been driven. One of these is known as Neal's ranch, or Jackass Meadows. From this point there were trails which could be followed, and this was the first sign of a return to the regions of civilization.

CHAPTER V.

THE BIG TREES.

The fact that, in addition to the Yosemite Valley, already described in the preceding pages, Congress has given to the State of California, to hold as a public park, one of the largest and finest groves of the so-called (*par excellence*) Big Trees, makes it incumbent on us to devote one chapter of the present volume to a statement of some of the most interesting facts concerning these truly remarkable productions of the vegetable kingdom. This we do the more readily, as it is astonishing how little that is really reliable is to be found in all that has been published about the Big Trees. No correct statement of their distribution or dimensions has appeared in print; and, if their age has been correctly stated in one or two scientific journals, no such information ever finds its way into the popular descriptions of this tree, which are repeated over and over again in contributions to newspapers, and in books of travel. For all the statements here made the Geological Survey is responsible, except when it is otherwise expressly stated. For the history of the botanical name of this species I am specially indebted to Professor Brewer, Botanist of the Survey, who has investigated this somewhat complicated subject with care and with access to all the authorities.

According to Mr. Hutchings's statement, the Calaveras Grove of Big Trees was the first one discovered by white men, and the date was the spring of 1852. The person who first stumbled on these vegetable monsters was Mr. A. T. Dowd, a hunter employed by the Union Water Company to supply the men in their employ with fresh meat, while digging a canal to bring water down to Murphy's. According to the accounts, the discoverer found that his story gained so little credence among the workmen that he was obliged to resort to a ruse to get them to the spot where the trees were.

The wonderful tale of the Big Trees soon found its way into the papers, and appears to have been first published in the Sonora Herald, the nearest periodical to the locality. The account was republished, among other papers, in the *Echo du Pacific* of San Francisco, then copied into the London Athenæum of July 23d, 1853 (p. 892), which is believed to be the first notice published in Europe, and from there again into the Gardener's Chronicle of London, where it appeared July 30th, 1853 (p. 488). In the last-named journal, for December 24th, page 819, Dr. Lindley published the first scientific description of the Big Tree. Overlooking its close affinity with the already described redwood, he regarded it as the type of a new genus, which he called *Wellingtonia*, adding the specific name of *gigantea*. His specimens were received from Mr. William Lobb, through Messrs. Veitch & Sons, well-known nurserymen. The tree had been previously brought to the notice of scientific men in San Francisco, and specimens had been sent to Dr. Torrey in New York considerably earlier than to Dr. Lindley, but the specimens were lost in transmission; and, no description having been published in San Francisco, although Drs. Kellogg and Behr had brought it to the notice of the California Academy early that year as a new species, the honor and opportunity of naming it was lost to American botanists. The closely allied species of the same genus, the *Sequoia sempervirens*, the redwood, had been named and described by Endlicher in 1847, and was well known to botanists all over the world in 1852.

At the meeting of the "Société Botanique de France," held June 28th, 1854, the eminent botanist Decaisne presented specimens of the two species, the Big Tree and the redwood, with those of other Californian *coniferæ*, recently received from the Consular Agent of France at San Francisco. At this meeting M. Decaisne gave his reasons, at some length, for considering the redwood and the more recently discovered "Big Tree" to belong to the same genus, *Sequoia*, and, in accordance with the rules of botanical nomenclature, called the new species *Sequoia gigantea*. The report of these proceedings is to be found in the *Bulletin de la Société Botanique de France*, Vol. I. p. 70, which was issued in July (probably) of 1854.

In the mean time specimens had been received by Dr. Torrey at New York, and in September of the same year (1854) Professor Gray, of Cambridge, published, in the American Journal of Science, appended to a notice of the age of the redwood, a statement, on his own authority, that a comparison of the cones of that tree and those of the so-called *Wellingtonia* of Lindley did not bring to view any differences adequate to the establishment of a new genus. To this Professor Gray adds: "The so-called *Wellingtonia* will hereafter bear the name imposed by Dr. Torrey, namely, that of *Sequoia gigantea*." It does not appear, however, on examination, that Dr. Torrey had himself published any description of the Big Tree, or of the fact that he considered it generically identical with the redwood, and priority seems to have been secured by Decaisne, so that the name must now stand as *Sequoia gigantea*, Decaisne. It is to the happy accident of the generic agreement of the Big Tree with the redwood that we owe it that we are not now obliged to call the largest and most interesting tree of America after an English military hero; had it been an English botanist of the highest eminence, the dose would not have been so unpalatable.

No other plant ever attracted so much attention or attained such a celebrity within so short a period. The references to it in scientific works and journals already number between one and two hundred, and it has been the theme of innumerable articles in popular periodicals and books of travel, in various languages; probably there is hardly a newspaper in Christendom that has not published some item on the subject.

Seeds were first sent to Europe and the Eastern States in 1853, and since that time immense numbers have found their way to market. They germinate readily, and it is probable that hundreds of thousands of the trees (millions it is said) are growing in different parts of the world from seeds planted. They flourish with peculiar luxuriance in Great Britain, and grow with extraordinary rapidity. Numerous examples are cited where they have grown over two feet per year, and have produced cones when four or five years old. Some marked "gardener's varieties" are already in the market.

The genus was named in honor of Sequoia[*] or Séquoyah, a Cherokee Indian of mixed blood, better known by his English name of George Guess, who is supposed to have been born about 1770, and who lived in Will's Valley, in the extreme northeastern corner of Alabama, among the Cherokees.

---

[*] Endlicher, who named the genus, was not only a learned botanist, but was eminent in ethnological research, and was undoubtedly well aquainted with Sequoia's career. The name is also, and more generally, spelt "Sequoyah," which is the English way of writing it, while the other is what it would naturally and properly be in Latin.

He became known to the world by his invention of an alphabet and written language for his tribe. This alphabet, which was constructed with wonderful ingenuity, consisted of eighty-six characters, each representing a syllable; and it had already come into use, to a considerable extent, before the whites had heard anything of it. After a time the missionaries took up Sequoyah's idea, and had types cast and a printing-press supplied to the Cherokee nation, and a newspaper was started in 1828, partly in this character. Driven with the rest of his tribe beyond the Mississippi, he died in New Mexico, in 1843. His remarkable alphabet is still in use, although destined to pass away with his nation, but not into oblivion, for his name attached to one of the grandest and most impressive productions of the vegetable kingdom will forever keep his memory green.*

Having given a few items in the history of the discovery of the Big Trees, we will pass on to detail some of the facts in regard to their geographical distribution, age, size, and appearance, with which it will be desirable for travellers to be acquainted.

The Big Tree is extremely limited in its range; even more so than its twin brother, the redwood. The latter is strictly a Coast Range or sea-board tree; the other inland, or exclusively limited to the Sierra. Both trees are, also, peculiarly Californian. A very few of the redwood may be found just across the border in Oregon, but the Big Tree has never been found outside of California, and probably never will be.†

The redwood forms an interrupted belt along the Coast Ranges, from about latitude 36° to 42°. or from a little below the head of the Nacimiento River, north to the northern boundary of the State. Between the southern termination of the belt and Carmelo, the redwoods occur but sparingly, nowhere forming extensive groves; and from Carmelo to the Pajaro River they are interrupted altogether. Near the last-named place this tree sets in again, and forms a tolerably continuous belt north to a point nearly opposite

---

* For the above particulars of Sequoyah's history, and several other items which we have not here space to publish, we are indebted to Professor Brewer.

† There are several *fossil* species of the genus *Sequoia*. The Miocene Tertiary of Greenland, in 70° north latitude, furnishes one, — the *Sequoia Langsdorffii* — which, according to the eminent botanist Heer, can with difficulty be distinguished from the redwood of California; it may, perhaps, be identical with it. The statement above, that the *Sequoia* is a peculiarly Californian genus, must be understood as referring to the vegetation of the present geological epoch, and not to that of former ages.

Half-Moon Bay, keeping well upon the western side of the ridges, but descending on the eastern side into the cañons. There were formerly fine redwoods opposite San Francisco, along the crest of the Contra Costa Hills; but they are now all cut down. The small patches of them in Marin County are fast going the same way. Beyond Russian River, however, the belt of redwoods widens out rapidly, forming almost a continuous forest, some ten or fifteen miles in width, up to the northern end of Mendocino County, or for more than a hundred miles. From here north, through Humboldt, Klamath, and Del Norte Counties, this tree occurs in more or less disconnected patches, some of which, however, cover an extensive area. In this direction the redwood gradually approaches the coast, and at Humboldt and Trinity Bays, and near Crescent City, is directly upon the ocean. Mr. Bolander thinks that his observations show clearly that the redwood is exclusively confined to a peculiar kind of rock, — the metamorphic sandstone, — and it is certain, also, that it will only flourish when it is frequently enveloped in the ocean fogs.

The redwood is the glory of the Coast Ranges; its gigantic size and its beauty of form and foliage entitle it to a place hardly second to that of the Big Tree itself, as may be gathered from the following facts derived chiefly from the notes of Messrs. Brewer and Bolander.

Near Santa Cruz is a redwood grove of great beauty; the largest tree is 50 feet in circumference at the base and 275 feet high. Near Crescent City Professor Brewer measured one 58 feet in circumference at four feet from the ground, and it scarcely swelled at all at its base. Several persons stated, however, that there were larger ones south of this, and that, near the Klamath River, there were some as much as 30 feet in diameter. Mr. Ashburner heard of a hollow redwood stump, seven miles back from Eureka, 38 feet in diameter, in which 33 pack-mules were corralled at one time. Mr. Bolander reported a redwood 25 feet in diameter, near Little River, Mendocino County.

During the stormy winter of 1861 – 62 immense numbers of redwood logs were carried out to sea, along the coast in the northern part of the State. They were so abundant as to be dangerous to ships at a distance of over 150 miles from land. During a heavy southwest gale great numbers of these were cast on shore near Crescent City, and thrown together in gigantic piles.

Professor Brewer measured a dozen of these broken, battered logs, and found them to vary from 120 to 210 feet in length; one of 200 feet was ten feet in diameter at the base, and another of 210 feet was three feet in diameter at the little end. Accurate measurements of the height of the trees standing in the forests of this region are wanting; but there are supposed to be many redwoods from 250 to 300 feet in elevation.

Thus we see, that in size the redwood falls but very little below the Big Tree, and it is not impossible that some of the former may yet be found as large as any of the latter. In general effect the forests of redwood, in the opinion of Professor Brewer, surpass even the groves of Big Trees. The great reason for this is, that the redwood forms frequently almost the entire forest, while the Big Tree nowhere occurs except scattered among other trees, and never in clusters or groups isolated from other species. Let one imagine an entire forest, extending as far as the eye can reach, of trees of from eight to twelve feet in diameter, and from 200 to 300 feet high, thickly grouped, their trunks marvellously straight, not branching until they reach from 100 to 150 feet above the ground, and then forming a dense canopy, which shuts out the view of the sky, the contrast of the bright cinnamon-colored trunks with the sombre deep yet brilliant green of the foliage, the utter silence of these forests, where often no sound can be heard except the low thunder of the breaking surf of the distant ocean, — let one picture to himself a scene like this, and he may perhaps receive a faint impression of the majestic grandeur of the redwood forests of California.

The Big Tree occurs exclusively in "groves," or scattered over limited areas, never forming groups by themselves, but always disseminated among a much larger number of trees of other kinds. These patches on which the Big Trees stand do not equal in area a hundredth part of that which the redwoods cover exclusively. We are quite unable to state the number of square miles or acres on which the Big Trees grow, except for two of the groves, the Calaveras and Mariposa, both of which have been carefully surveyed by our parties. It may be roughly stated, however, that this area does not, so far as yet known, exceed fifty square miles, and that most of this is in one patch, between King's and Kaweah Rivers, as will be noticed farther on.

The groves of the Big Trees are limited in latitude between 36° and

38° 15′ nearly, at least so far as we now know. The Calaveras Grove is the most northerly, and one on the south fork of the Tule is the farthest south of any yet known to us. They are also quite limited in vertical range, since they nowhere descend much below 5,000 or rise above 7,000 feet. They follow the other trees of California, in this respect, that they occur lower down on the Sierra as we go northwards; the most northerly grove, that of Calaveras, is the lowest in elevation above the sea-level.

We will first describe, or notice, so far as our space allows, the different groves which have been discovered, giving more details of that one which has been given by Congress to the State of California "for public use and recreation," and we will then state some general facts connected with this species, which will be better understood after reading what has preceded.

There are eight distinct patches or groves of the Big Trees, — or nine, if we should consider the Mariposa trees as belonging to two different groups, which is hardly necessary, inasmuch as there is only a ridge half a mile in width separating the upper grove from the lower. The eight groves are, in geographical order from north to south: first, the Calaveras; second, the Stanislaus; third, Crane Flat; fourth, Mariposa; fifth, Fresno; sixth, King's and Kaweah Rivers; seventh, North Fork Tule River; eighth, South Fork Tule River. These we will now notice in the above order, beginning with the one best known and most visited.

The Calaveras Grove is situated in the county of that name, about sixteen miles from Murphy's Camp, and near the Stanislaus River. It is on, or near, the road crossing the Sierra by the Silver Mountain Pass. This being the first grove of the Big Trees discovered, and the most accessible, it has come more into notice and been much more visited than any of the others; indeed, this and the Mariposa Grove are the only ones which have become a resort for travellers. The Calaveras Grove has also the great advantage over the others, that a good hotel is kept there, and that it is accessible on wheels, all the others being at a greater or less distance from any road.

This grove occupies a belt 3,200 feet long by 700 feet broad, extending in a northwest and southeast direction, in a depression between two slopes, through which meanders a small brook which dries up in the summer. There are between 90 and 100 trees of large size in the grove, and a considerable number of small ones, chiefly on the outskirts. Several have fallen since the grove was discovered; one has been cut down; and one has had the bark stripped from it up to the height of 116 feet above the ground. The bark thus removed was exhibited in different places, and finally found a resting-place in the Sydenham Crystal Palace, where it was unfortunately burned, in the fire which consumed a part of that building a few years since. The two trees thus destroyed were perhaps the finest in the grove; the tallest now standing is the one called the "Keystone State"; the largest and finest is known as the "Empire State." The height of this grove above the sea-level is 4,759 feet.

The annexed table shows the elevation of all the trees which could be conveniently measured, and their circumference at six feet above the ground: —

TABLE OF MEASUREMENTS OF HEIGHT AND CIRCUMFERENCE OF TREES IN THE CALAVERAS GROVE.

Name of Tree.	Circumference 6 feet above ground.	Height.
	Feet.	Feet.
Keystone State	45	325
General Jackson	40	319
Mother of the Forest.....(without bark)	61	315
Daniel Webster	47	307
Richard Cobden	41	284
T. Starr King	52	283
Pride of the Forest	48	282
Henry Clay	47	280
Bay State	46	275
Jas. King of William	51	274
Sentinel	49	272
Dr. Kane	50	271
Arborvitæ Queen	30	269
Abraham Lincoln	44	268
Maid of Honor	27	266
Old Vermont	40	265
Uncle Sam	43	265
Mother & Son (Mother)	51	261
Three Graces (highest)	30	262
Wm. Cullen Bryant	48	262
U. S. Grant	34	261
General Scott	43	258
George Washington	51	256
Henry Ward Beecher	34	252
California	33	250
Uncle Tom's Cabin	50	250
Beauty of the Forest	39	249
J. B. M'Pherson	31	246
Florence Nightingale	37	246
James Wadsworth	27	239
Elihu Burritt	31	231

The exact measurement of the diameter and the ascertaining of the age of one of the largest trees in this grove was made possible by cutting it down. This was done soon after the grove was discovered, and is said to have occupied five men during twenty-two days. The felling was done by boring through the tree with pump-augers; it was no small affair to persuade the trunk to fall, even after it had been completely severed from its connection with the base. It was done, however, by driving in wedges on one side, until the ponderous mass was inclined sufficiently, which was not effected until after three days of labor.

The stump of this tree was squared off smoothly at six feet above the ground, and the bark being removed, a pavilion was built over it, forming a capacious room, the exact dimensions of the stump inside of the bark being,

Across its longest diameter, south of centre,	13 feet	9½ inches.
" " " north of centre,	10 "	4 "
Total longest diameter . .	24 "	1½ "

The shorter diameter, or that east and west, was 23 feet, divided exactly even on each side of the centre. The thickness of the bark, averaging 18 inches probably, would add three feet to the diameter of the tree, making 27 feet in all. After this tree had been cut down, it was again cut through about 30 feet from the first cut. At the upper end of this section of the trunk, or about 40 feet from the ground, as the tree originally stood, we carefully counted the rings of annual growth, measuring at the same time the width of each set of one hundred, beginning at the exterior; the result was as follows:—

First hundred....................	3.0 inches.
Second "	3.7 "
Third "	4.1 "
Fourth "	3.9 "
Fifth "	4.1 "
Sixth "	4.1 "
Seventh "	4.6 "
Eighth "	5.6 "
Ninth "	7.3 "
Tenth "	7.9 "
Eleventh "	10.1 "
Twelfth "	13.0 "
55 years "	9.4 "
1,255 years.	80.8 "

There was a small cavity in the centre of the tree which prevented an accurate fixing of its age; but making due allowance for that, and for the time required to grow to the height at which the count was made, it will be safe to say that this particular tree, which was probably about as large as any now standing in the grove, was, in round numbers, 1,300 years old.

The Calaveras Grove contains, as will be seen in the table on page 146, four trees over 300 feet high, the highest one measured in the Mariposa Grove being 272. The published statements of the heights of these trees are considerably exaggerated, as will be noticed; but our measurements can be relied on as being correct.* The Keystone State has the honor of standing at the head, with 325 feet as its elevation, and this is the tallest tree yet measured on this continent, so far as our information goes. When we observe how regularly and gradually the trees diminish in size, from the highest down, it will be evident that the stories told, of trees having once stood in this grove over 400 feet in height, are not entitled to credence. It is not at all likely that any one tree should have overtopped all the others by 75 feet or more. The same condition of general average elevation, and absence of trees very much taller than any of the rest in the grove, will be noticed among the trees on the Mariposa grant, where, however, there is no one as high as 300 feet.

The next grove south of the one just noticed is south of the Stanislaus River, near the borders of Calaveras and Tuolumne Counties. It has never been visited by any member of the Geological Survey, and is not located on any map. It has been described to us as being about ten miles southeast of the Calaveras Grove, on Beaver Creek, a branch of the Stanislaus. It is said to contain from 600 to 800 trees, but none as large as those already described.

About twenty-five miles southeast of the last-mentioned grove is another, which may be called the Crane Flat Grove, as it is from a mile to a mile and a half from the station of that name on the Coulterville trail to the Yosemite, in a northwesterly direction. It was visited by our party, in haste, and its extent was not ascertained nor the number of trees counted. They stand mostly on the north slope of a hill, rather sheltered from the wind;

---

* Several trees were measured twice, and the results, in every case, found to be closely coincident.

and, so far as observed, are rather smaller than those of the Calaveras Grove. The largest sound tree measured was 57 feet in circumference, at three feet from the ground. A stump, so burned that only one half remained, was 23 feet in diameter, inside the bark at three feet from the ground. A single Big Tree stands in the woods, by itself, somewhere southwest of the Crane Flat Grove, and between it and the Merced. It is the only instance, so far as we know, of the occurrence of this species thus solitary and alone. There is an almost entirely unexplored region between the Beaver Creek and the Crane Flat Groves, and there may possibly be some more Big Trees existing there and not yet discovered. It is about twenty miles, still in a southwesterly direction, from Crane Flat to the Mariposa Grove, and that region has been so thoroughly explored by the Survey, that there is no reason to suppose that any more of these trees will be found there.

The Mariposa Grove is situated about sixteen miles directly south of the Lower Hotel in the Yosemite Valley, and between three and four miles southeast of Clark's ranch, and at an elevation of about 1,500 feet above the last-named place, or of 5,500 feet above the sea-level. It lies in a little valley, occupying a depression on the back of a ridge, which runs along in an easterly direction between Big Creek and the South Merced. One of the branches of the creek heads in the grove.

The grant made by Congress is two miles square, and embraces, in reality, two distinct, or nearly distinct groves; that is to say, two collections of Big Trees, between which there is an intervening space without any. The Upper Grove is in a pretty compact body, containing, on an area of 3,700 by 2,300 feet in dimensions, just 365 trees of the *Sequoia gigantea*, of a diameter of one foot and over, besides a great number of small ones. The lower grove, which is smaller in size and more scattered, lies in a southwesterly direction from the other, some trees growing quite high up in the gulches on the south side of the ridge which separates the two groves.

The trail approaches the Upper Grove from the west side, and passes through and around it, in such a manner as to take the visitor very near to almost all the largest trees; to accomplish this, it ascends one branch of the creek and then crosses over and descends the other, showing that the size of the trees depends somewhat on their position in regard to water. Still, there are several very large ones on the side hill south of the creek, quite high above the water.

Several of the trees in this grove have been named, some of them, indeed, half a dozen times; there are no names, however, which seem to have become current, as is the case in the Calaveras Grove. A plan has been drawn for the Commissioners, however, showing each tree, with its exact position and size, a number being attached to each. The circumference of every tree in the grove was also carefully measured, and the height of such as could be conveniently got at for this purpose.

From the following table it will be seen that there are several trees in this grove larger than any in the Calaveras, and that their average size is greater. The average height of the Mariposa trees, however, is less than that of the Calaveras; and the highest of the former, 272 feet, is 53 feet less than the tallest one of the latter. There is a burned stump on the north side of the grove, nearly all gone, but indicating a tree of a size perhaps a little greater than any now existing here. The beauty of the Mariposa Grove has been sadly marred by the ravages of fire, which has evidently swept through it again and again, almost ruining many of the finest trees. Still, the general appearance of the grove is extremely grand and imposing. There are about 125 trees over 40 feet in circumference.

The principal trees associated with the Big Trees in this grove are: the pitch and sugar pines, the Douglas spruce, the white fir (*Picea grandis*), and the bastard cedar (*Libocedrus decurrens*); the latter so much resembles the Big Tree in the general appearance of its trunk and bark, that there was no person in our party who could certainly distinguish the two species at a little distance.

There are but very few of the young Big Trees growing within the grove, where probably they have been destroyed by fire; around the base of several of the large trees, on the outskirts of the grove, there are small plantations of young *Sequoias*, of all sizes, up to six or eight inches in diameter, but only a few as large as this. Those trees which are about ten feet in diameter and entirely uninjured by fire, in the full symmetry of a vigorous growth of say 500 years, are, although not as stupendous as the older giants of the forest, still exceedingly beautiful and impressive.

The annexed table gives the height of all that were measured, and the circumference of these and of several other of the largest trees in the grove, with some remarks as to their condition and appearance: —

TABLE OF MEASUREMENTS OF HEIGHT AND CIRCUMFERENCE OF TREES IN THE MARIPOSA GROVE.

No.	Height.	Circumference at Ground.	Circumference at 6 feet above the Ground.	Remarks.
6		77.5		
7		72.5		
11		62.		
12	244	62.	....	Very fine symmetrical tree.
15	272	....	....	Fine sound tree.
16	...	86.5	....	31 feet in diameter. Hollow.
20	...	72.5	55.	Fine tree.
21	...	....	44.	Very fine tree, not swollen at base.
27	250	48.		
29	...	89.8		
31	186	35.7	29.6	Very straight and symmetrical.
35	...	65.	50.8	
38	226	27.		
49	194			
51	218	56.	39.	Very fine tree.
52	249	....	40.	Fine tree.
60	...	81.6	59.	Very fine tree, but burned at base.
64	...	82.4	50.	Very fine tree.
66	221	39.8		
69	219	35.7		
70	225	43.9		
77	197	....	27.8	
102	255	...	50.	Very fine tree.
158	223			
164	243		27.6	
169	...	79.6	....	Much burned at base.
171	...	82.7	....	Badly burned on one side.
174	268	....	40.8	
194	192	....	46.	Two trees, united at the base.
205	229	87.8		Much burned on one side, formerly over 100 feet in circumference.
206	235	70.4		
216	...	....	63.2	Very large tree, much burned at base.
226	219	....	48.	Fine tree.
236	256	....	46.	
238	...	....	57.	26 feet in diameter, burned on one side.
239	187	....	26.6	
245	270	81.6	67.2	Burned on one side.
253	...	74.3	60.	
262	...	56.	....	Half burned away at base.
275	...	68.		
286	...	76.	....	Burned on one side nearly to centre.
290	...	....	46.	
301	...	...	51.	Largest tree in the Grove, 27 feet in diameter, but all burned away on one side.
304	260	92.7		
330		91.6		Splendid tree, over 100 feet in circumference originally, but much burned at base.
348	227	....	51.	

The meadows on the Big Tree Grant abound in gay, blooming flowers. Mr. Bolander enumerates, as the most conspicuous: *Rudbeckia Californica*,

Gray; *Aconitum nasutum*, Fischer; *Anisocarpus Bolanderi*, Gray; *Boykinia occidentalis*, T. and G.; *Sidalcea malvæflora*, Gray; *Myrica Gale*, L.; *Hulsia brevifolia*, Gray; *Epilobium angustifolium*; *Veratrum Californicum*. A species of lupine is very abundant, and this, with the *Rudbeckia*, gives the main coloring to the meadows, which also abound with numerous carices.

The southern division of the Mariposa Grove, or Lower Grove, as it is usually called, is said to contain about half as many trees as the one just described. They are much scattered among other trees, and do not, therefore, present as imposing an appearance as those in the other grove, where quite a large number can often be seen from one point. The largest tree in the Lower Grove is the one known as the "Grizzly Giant," which is 93 feet 7 inches in circumference at the ground, and 64 feet 3 inches at 11 feet above. Its two diameters at the base, as near as we could measure, were 30 and 31 feet. The calculated diameter, at 11 feet above the ground, is 20 feet nearly. The tree is very much injured and decreased in size by burning, for which no allowance has been made in the above measurements. Some of the branches of this tree are fully six feet in diameter, or as large as the trunks of the largest elms of the Connecticut Valley, of which Dr. Holmes has so pleasantly discoursed in the Atlantic Monthly. This tree, however, has long since passed its prime, and has the battered and war-worn appearance conveyed by its name.

The next grove south of the Mariposa is one in Fresno County, about fourteen miles southeast of Clark's, and not far from a conspicuous point called Wammelo Rock. Mr. Clark has described this grove, which we have not visited, as extending for above two and a half miles in length by from one to two in breadth. He has counted 500 trees in it, and believes the whole number to be not far from 600. The largest measured 81 feet in circumference, at three feet from the ground.

No other grove of Big Trees has been discovered to the southeast of this, along the slope of the Sierra, until we reach a point more than fifty miles distant from the Fresno Grove. Here, between the King's and Kaweah Rivers, is by far the most extensive collection of trees of this species which has yet been discovered in the State.

This belt of trees, for grove it can hardly be called, occurs about thirty miles north-northeast of Visalia, on the tributaries of the King's and Kaweah

Rivers, and on the divide between. They are scattered over the slopes and on the valleys, but are larger in the depressions, where the soil is more moist. Along the trail which runs from Visalia to the Big Meadows, the belt is four or five miles wide, and it extends over a vertical range of about 2,500 feet; its total length is as much as eight or ten miles, and may be more. The trees are not collected together into groves, but are scattered through the forests, and associated with the other species usually occurring at this altitude in the Sierra: they are most abundant at from 6,000 to 7,000 feet elevation above the sea-level. Their number is great; probably thousands might be counted. Their size, however, is not great, the average being from ten to twelve feet in diameter, and but few exceeding 20 feet; but smaller trees are very numerous. One tree, which had been cut, had a diameter of eight feet, exclusive of the bark, and was 377 years old. The largest one seen was near Thomas's Mill; this had a circumference of 106 feet near the ground, no allowance being made for a portion which was burned away at the base. When entire the tree may have been ten or twelve feet more in circumference. At about twelve feet from the ground, the circumference was 75 feet. Its height was 276 feet. The top was dead, however, and, although the tree was symmetrical and in good growth, it had past its prime.

Another tree, which had fallen, and had been burned hollow, was so large, that three horsemen could ride abreast into the cavity for a distance of 30 feet, its height and width being about 11 feet. At a distance of 70 feet the diameter of the cavity was still as much as eight feet. The base of this tree could not be easily measured; but the trunk was burned through at 120 feet from the ground, and at that point had a diameter (exclusive of the bark) of 13 feet 2 inches; and, at 169 feet from its base, the tree was nine feet in diameter. The Indians stated that a still larger tree existed to the north of King's River. This tree should be looked up and carefully measured; unfortunately, it was not in the power of our party to do this.

All through these forests there are numerous young Big Trees, of all sizes, from the seedling upwards, and at Thomas's mill they are cut up for lumber, in a manner quite at variance with the oft-repeated story of the exceptional character of the species. Prostrate trunks of old trees are also numerous;

some of them must have lain for ages, as they were nearly gone, while the wood is very durable.

The only other groves yet discovered are those on the Tule River, of which there are two, one on the north and the other on the south branch of that stream. They are 15 miles apart, and the most northerly of the two is about 30 miles from the grove last described. As the intervening region has been but little explored, it is not at all unlikely that more of the Big Trees may be found along the fork of the Kaweah which intersects this region with its numerous branches. We are not aware that these two Tule groves were known previous to their discovery by Mr. D'Heureuse, one of the topographers of the Geological Survey, in 1867; at least, no notice of them had ever appeared in print. The number of trees in these groves is quite large, as they are scattered over several square miles of area. The largest of them were said by Mr. D'Heureuse to be about the size of the largest in the other groves.

Not one of the Big Trees has ever been found south of the grove on the South Fork of the Tule. The region has not, however, been so thoroughly explored that it would be safe to say that none exist there. Judging from the extent of the area over which this species is scattered, between King's and Kaweah Rivers, it would seem that here was its most congenial habitat, and it may eventually be found that this tree forms pretty nearly a continuous belt, for some fifty or sixty miles.

From what has been stated above, the reader will easily gather, that the Big Tree is not that wonderfully exceptional thing which popular writers have almost always described it as being. It is not so restricted in its range as some other species of the *Coniferæ* in California; it occurs in great abundance, of all ages and sizes, and there is no reason to suppose that it is now dying out, or that it belongs to a past geological era, any more than the redwood. The age of the Big Trees is not so great as that assigned, by the highest authorities, to some of the English yews. Neither is its height as great, by far, as that of an Australian species, the *Eucalyptus amygdalina*, many of which have, on the authority of Dr. Müller, the eminent Government botanist, been found to measure over 400 feet. One, indeed, reaches the enormous elevation of 480 feet, thus overtopping the tallest *Sequoia* by 155 feet. There are also trees which exceed the Big Tree in diameter, as, for instance, the Baobab (*Adansonia digitata*); but these are always comparatively low, not exceeding 60 or 70 feet in height, and much swollen at the base.

On the whole, it may be stated, that there is no known tree which approaches the *Sequoia* in grandeur, thickness, and height, being both taken into consideration, unless it be the *Eucalyptus*. The largest Australian tree yet reported is said to be 81 feet in circumference, at four feet from the ground; this is nearly, but not quite, as large as some of the largest of the Big Trees of California.

THE END.

University Press, Cambridge: Printed by Welch, Bigelow, & Co.

www.ingramcontent.com/pod-product-compliance
Lightning Source LLC
Chambersburg PA
CBHW032155160426
43197CB00008B/932